Fedayeen

By the same author

Middle East Journey
Return to Glory
One Man's War
    (*Angus & Robertson*)
Digger (The Story of the Australian Soldier)
Scotland the Brave (The Story of the Scottish Soldier)
Jackboot (The Story of the German Soldier)
Tommy Atkins (The Story of the English Soldier)
Jack Tar (The Story of the English Seaman)
    (*Cassell*)
The Face of War
British Campaign Medals
Codes and Ciphers
Anzacs at War
Boys in Battle
Women in Battle
    (*Abelard-Schuman*)
The Walking Wounded (*Amalgamated Press*)
Links of Leadership (*Harrap*)
Swifter than Eagles (Biography of Marshal of the R.A.F. Sir John
    Salmond) (*Blackwood*)
Surgeons in the Field
Americans in Battle
Letters from the Front 1914-18
    (*Dent*)

The Hunger to Come (Food and Population Crises)
New Geography 1966-7
New Geography 1968-9
New Geography 1970-1
Anatomy of Captivity (Political Prisoners)
    (*Abelard-Schuman*)
Devil's Goad (*Dent*)
And other titles

Fedayeen

The Arab-Israeli Dilemma

John Laffin

CASSELL · LONDON

CASSELL & COMPANY LTD
35 Red Lion Square, London WC1R 4SG
Sydney, Auckland
Toronto, Johannesburg

First published 1973
ISBN 0 304 29189 7

PRINTED IN GREAT BRITAIN BY
NORTHUMBERLAND PRESS LTD., GATESHEAD

F 173

Contents

Illustrations

Acknowledgments

Some of my sources must remain anonymous for their own safety but many can be named and thanked for personal interviews or my use of their written work. Inevitably, there are more Arabs in the list than others because the fedayeen *are* Arab and they operate from an Arab environment.

Principal Arab authorities:

Dr. Sonia Hamady, Dr. Hisham Sharabi, editor of *Journal of Palestine Studies*; George Antonius, Miss Thurayya Antonius, secretary of the Fifth of June Society; Abu Ayad (Salah Halef), Mrs. Khalidi El-Fattal, editor of *Arab World*; Nasir ad-Din an-Nashashibi, Walid Khadduri, director, Institute of Palestine Studies; Clovis Maksoud, Naji Alush, Sabri Jiryis, Mohammed Heikal, Ibrahim Al-Abid, executive secretary PLO Research Centre; Hazim al-Khalidi, Lutfi al-Khouli, Nabil Khury, Dr. Yusif Sayegh, Dr. Nabil Sh'at, Leila S. Kadi, Mahmoud Abu Zeluf, Edmund Ghareeb, Aref el-Aref, Ghassan Kanafani, Ahmed Jamal, Dr. Walid Khalidi, President of the Institute of Palestine Studies; Mrs. Walid Khalidi.

Principal Israeli authorities:

Dr. Yehoshafat Harkabi, one-time chief of Israeli Intelligence; Elie Landau, Professor Shimon Shamir, Dr. Joshua

Porat, General Shlomo Gazit, Dan Shiftan, Ehud Yaari, Shabtai Teveth, Gideon Weigert, Jon and David Kimche, Dafna Allon, Oded Eran, Professor Theodor Meron.

Foreign authorities:

This list does not include newspaper writers already mentioned in the text, and to whom I extend my professional thanks. Gerard Chaliand, John Reddaway, C.M.G., O.B.E., Sir John Glubb, Hal Draper, Mrs. M. Kennedy, Ernest Stock, Henry Cattan, Professor P. J. Vatikiotis, Jac Weller, Brigadier Peter Young, Evan Wilson, the Very Rev. George Appleton, Anglican Archbishop in Jerusalem.

I am grateful to officials of UNRWA for certain assistance and to diplomats of several nationalities for their unofficial opinions on the fedayeen–Israel dispute. My thanks must go, too, to many Palestinians in UNRWA camps and ordinary villages, and to Israelis in kibbutz and town. Without their impression a balanced view would be impossible to obtain. I appreciate the help of the Director and staff of, respectively, the Institute for Palestine Studies, Beirut, the Council for the Advancement of Arab–British Understanding, London, the Truman Institute, Jerusalem. Personally I owe much to my wife for her researches, particularly in Lebanon and Israel, and for much other work on my behalf. Without her help this book would have been difficult to finish.

The Palestinian Fedayeen
An Introduction

This is the story of the Palestinian organisations operating against Israel. Its members refer to themselves as guerrillas, commandos, partisans, freedom, resistance or liberation fighters, and avengers. The Israelis label them saboteurs, terrorists, criminals, malcontents and thugs. The world's information media has seized on the most colourful terms and indiscriminately uses the terms 'guerrilla' or 'terrorist', though the label sometimes depends on politics. For instance, in much of Africa the Palestinians are liberation heroes; in most of Europe they are terrorists while in certain Arab countries they are denounced as 'traitors'.

A writer who is neither Arab nor Jew and who does not wish to give the impression that he is a propagandist for either Palestinians or Israelis cannot use any of these terms as his own. This would be implicit acceptance of the bias each of them proclaims or of the inaccurate definition of some of them. For instance, the term guerrilla is not acceptable, for such a fighter is an irregular soldier who wages war independently. Guerrilla war is, by definition, an internal war, a condition of domestic disruption or civil disturbance. A hit-and-run attack on Israeli-occupied territories or in Israel itself, mounted from other countries, is not guerrilla warfare. The Palestinian qualifies as a guerrilla only if, for instance, the planned blowing up of buses carrying school children is 'waging war' in the accepted sense. Terminology should not be stretched to the point of distortion.

Fedayeen

'Commando' was a popular word, for a time, in the Western news media. It is highly misleading, since a commando—again by definition—is a regular soldier waging regular war. The only difference between the commando and the ordinary soldier is one of quality. Commando raids are usually meticulously planned *military* operations. Sporadic terror acts—the throwing of the odd hand grenade, the occasional placing of a time bomb in the dustbins of public places, or the firing of long-range Katyusha rockets from across frontiers—are not commando-type military operations.

The Israelis commonly describe the Palestinian fighters as terrorists. In that terrorists have no specific military target and do not care who is killed by the bomb left in a cafeteria the term is apt enough. But it is misleading if only because it invites the false conclusion that terror is evident in Israel. In any case, the word has emotive, abusive connotations which are a barrier to objectivity.

Also, the fine line between terrorism and resistance—the former being the application of violence against the rights of other people, the latter violence used to defend threatened or usurped rights—is easily distorted.

The armed activities of the Palestine 'Liberation' Movement from 1965 to 1972 were, for purposes of classification, somewhere between those of guerrillas and regular army infiltrations of enemy occupied territories.

For the sake of objectivity I use the term fedayeen throughout this book, except where I quote terms used by other people. The name is in common use in Arabic—and has been adopted by most Arabic newspapers—for Arab irregulars operating against Israel and against 'reactionary' Arab states. The word comes from the root 'sacrifice', that is, those who sacrifice themselves or embark on a suicidal mission. Historically, the name was given in the twelfth century to those selected to assassinate the enemies of the Isma'ili sect—the Assassins. In the context of the Arab–Israeli conflict the name fedayeen

xii

became prominent in 1955 when the Egyptian authorities organised and despatched 'irregulars' on subversive missions to Israel.

The Palestinian fedayeen are different from the Egyptians, especially in motivation, but very similar to the ancient Arabs in their dedication to assassination. The connotation of sacrifice is fitting for many lives have been lost, though it is doubtful if the Palestinians' sacrifice is voluntary in the accepted sense. Many rank-and-file fedayeen have been sacrificed in a complexity of political intrigue they could hardly comprehend.

I have drawn on Arab and Israeli sources for material as I have friends—some of them close friends—on either side of that unhappy border of mistrust and misunderstanding—scholars, generals, fedayeen leaders, leading citizens, ordinary Palestinian Arabs and ordinary Israeli Jews. All have been remarkably frank. Leaders on both sides have given me access to records and to people usually kept protected from the questions of a writer. I am grateful for their belief in my impartiality and must say that I have not knowingly revealed secrets entrusted to me as such. At the same time, I have not felt inhibited in using any information which has come to me through my own investigations. There is, in this book, much that has not before been revealed.

My book has four principal purposes: To examine the rise of the fedayeen movement to the peak of its success and decline; to show the significance of the movement to both Arabs and Jews; to separate myth from reality; to account for the remarkable treatment given the fedayeen by the world's news media. This book does *not* purport to be analysis of the general rights and wrongs of the Arab–Israeli conflict—this is available elsewhere—but something definitive must be said about the Palestinian refugees, though much has been published about their plight. The original refugees are the Arabs who, as a result of the Arab–Israeli conflict in Palestine during 1948, left their homes in the territory which is now Israel and took refuge in neighbouring areas. By 1967 they, with their children, numbered about 1,300,000, but only 40 per cent were in UNRWA (United Nations Relief and Works Agency) camps. About 80 per cent were farmers and unskilled workers, and their families; the other 20 per cent were business and professional men, and their families. When war broke out again in 1967 tens of thousands of Arab families fled from their homes and sought refuge in east Jordan, Syria and Egypt. Some became refugees for the second time; for instance, among the people displaced from south-west Syria 17,500 were UNRWA-registered refugees. In 1971 3 per cent of the total population of Syria were registered refugees; in Lebanon the figure was 8 per cent; in both east Jordan and the West Bank about 35 per cent and in the Gaza Strip, 66 per cent.

It is from among the Palestinians who live outside the borders of Israel that most fedayeen have come. A vast amount of published material—clear fact and blatant propaganda—is available to anybody intent on trying to follow the tortuous convolutions of the fedayeen movement. Inevitably, much of it is biased—if only by the process of selectivity. Even scholars of the reputation of Dr. Hisham Sharabi and Dr. Yehoshafat Harkabi—Arab and Jew respectively—cannot eradicate in their writings and sayings a subjective sensitivity and defensiveness.

From this mass of material and from my conversations on the spot with people who have experienced the events recorded, I have sought to unravel the story of the fedayeen. If some of my conclusions offend either Palestinian or Israeli I contend that the truth which has emerged from my researches should be told, for truth is a major step towards reality and reality is the basis of reconciliation.

JOHN LAFFIN

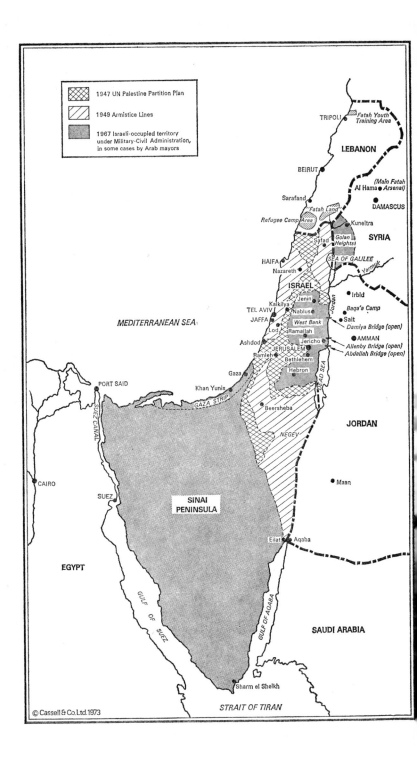

1947 UN Palestine Partition Plan

1949 Armistice Lines

1967 Israeli-occupied territory under Military-Civil Administration, in some cases by Arab mayors

TRIPOLI
Fatah Youth Training Area

LEBANON

BEIRUT

(Main Fatah Al Hama Arsenal)

Sarafand

DAMASCUS

"Fatah Land"

Refugee Camp Area

Kuneitra

SYRIA

Safad
Golan Heights

HAIFA

SEA OF GALILEE

Nazareth

Yarmuk

ISRAEL

Irbid

Jenin

Kalkilya

Nablus

Baqa'a Camp

TEL AVIV

JAFFA

West Bank

Salt

Jordan

Damiya Bridge (open)

Lod

Ramallah

Ashdod

JERUSALEM

Jericho

AMMAN

Allenby Bridge (open)

Ramleh

Bethlehem

Abdallah Bridge (open)

MEDITERRANEAN SEA

Hebron

Gaza

DEAD SEA

PORT SAID

Khan Yunis

GAZA STRIP

Beersheba

JORDAN

NEGEV

CAIRO

Maan

SUEZ CANAL

SUEZ

SINAI PENINSULA

Eilat Aqaba

EGYPT

GULF OF SUEZ

GULF OF AQABA

SAUDI ARABIA

Sharm el Sheikh

© Cassell & Co. Ltd. 1973

STRAIT OF TIRAN

1 *The Seeds of Sabotage*

On the night of January 2, 1965 three armed men in makeshift uniform and wearing the Arab *kaffiya* head-dress crossed the Jordan River at a shallow ford and made their shadowy way to the Israeli National Carrier water-canal in the Beit Netopha Valley.* Avoiding Israeli border guards, they reached the canal and placed an explosive charge of ten gelignite sticks. By dawn they were back in Jordanian territory, exhausted but jubilant—and probably unaware that their act was the signal for the beginning of a new form of conflict with Israel.

Their mission, in itself, was not successful. A water company worker discovered the gelignite about noon and at once radioed Control to ask that the water level be lowered. He then removed the inexpertly placed detonators. Border guards followed the tracks of the intruders to the Jordan and found the trodden reeds which betrayed their point of entry. But at that time the Israelis considered the border inviolable and the border patrol drove away.

The Arabs from across the river were led by Ahmed Musah and were fedayeen and members of Fatah, the largest of the many Palestinian–Arab underground organisations with anti-Israel policies. Fatah called the incident 'the opening shot in

* The Israeli National Water Carrier was a major Arab–Israel issue. In August 1963 the Arab governments and press became hysterical on hearing that Israel was completing a project for pumping water from the Sea of Galilee to the Negev desert.

1

the Palestinian Revolution', but while it was a 'non-exploit' it brought Fatah into the prominence of world headlines.*

As it happened, Ahmed Musah and his comrades ran into a Jordanian patrol. They refused to hand over their weapons and in a brief fight Musah was killed, so ironically Fatah's first casualty was at the hands of other Arabs, but the disaster which befell the party of fedayeen was not revealed for another 18 months so that fedayeen morale would not suffer.

In the brief period since January 1965 Fatah and its sister groups have fascinated the world with their exploits, thrown the Arab community into turmoil, irritated the Israelis and have been bloodily crushed—not by their Jewish enemies but by fellow Arabs. Fedayeen leaders, colourful and violent men, have demanded and received prominence. With a confidence amounting to effrontery Fatah, on October 15, 1968, submitted a statement to the General Assembly in which it rejected Israeli sovereignty in Palestine.

The fedayeen story is an extraordinary contrast of success and failure. They aroused the world's sympathy—and then alienated most of it. They raised the flag of Arab unity—and then trampled it in the sand. They succeeded in drawing to the Middle East the press of the world—but failed to inspire their own people. They startled the Arab community—but could not frighten the Israelis, though they believed they did so at the Battle of Karamah, March 21, 1968. By 1972 they had deteriorated from dedication to desperation and pathos had replaced pride.

The incident of January 3, 1965—which told the perceptive Israelis that they had another major problem on their hands —had roots 17 years old. From the time of the establishment of the State of Israel in 1948 Arab political publications stressed

* A more recent Fatah document claims that the first clash took place on August 18, 1964, when fedayeen on a reconnaissance mission near Gesher, a kibbutz in the Jordan Valley, ran into Israeli soldiers. A Fatah leader, Abu Ayad, has said that the first casualty was Khalid al-Hajj, killed on November 2, 1964, in an unplanned clash with an Israeli patrol.

that the Palestinian problem was of the gravest consequence for *all* Arabs.

Repeatedly Arab press and radio, politicians and even university professors, had demanded the overthrow of Israel by force, in language generally as violent as the deeds they advocated. They use many undisguised expressions of objective. 'Liquidation' has the highest frequency but other common phrases are 'wiping out', 'purification' or 'cleansing', 'throwing into the sea', 'throttling' or 'crushing', 'pulling up by the root'. 'God has gathered the Zionists together from the corners of the world so that the Arabs can kill them all at one stroke', said Ibrahim Tahwi, Assistant Secretary of the 'Liberation Rally'.*

It is not surprising that in the mid-1950s many young men from middle-class families were swayed by rhetoric and mock-rhetoric concerning 'resistance to Israeli occupation of Palestine'. Fluent in European languages—most of the founders of the fedayeen organisations were students of Egyptian universities—they read much about the resistance movements in Europe against the Nazis and liked to find parallels between their own situation and that of underground liberation movements in France, Italy, Poland, Czechoslovakia, Yugoslavia, the Soviet Union and Rumania. They saw the Algerians, in 1962, successfully rid themselves of French domination but did not see the profound differences between the Algerian and Palestinian situations. Britain was granting independence to former colonies—further encouragement to men who felt themselves the 'victims of imperialism'.

These potential leaders, their ambitions and intellectualism exasperated and frustrated by centuries of Arab technological backwardness, began to play with heady ideas—the resurgence of Arabism, the restoration of Arab glory. Such ideals need a cause on which to take root, and Palestine was the obvious choice. Israel, these young men claim, had dispossessed more

* Reported in the Cairo daily, *Al-Ahram*, September 8, 1956.

than a million Palestinian Arabs in 1948. They set themselves the mission of 'liberating' Palestine and restoring it to the Arabs. They also had to wipe out the shame suffered by the Arab states, which were decisively beaten when they tried to destroy Israel in the war of 1948—the war which the Israelis call their War of Independence.

It is difficult to be precise about who the Palestinians were, politically speaking, at this time, for Arab leaders and thinkers after World War I saw Palestine simply as part of Syria. Writing in 1938, George Antonius, the Arab historian, stipulated that: 'Except where otherwise specified the term Syria will be used to denote the whole of the country of that name which is now split into mandated territories of (French) Syria and the Lebanon and (British) Palestine and Trans-jordan.'*

The Grand Mufti of Jerusalem, Haj Amin el-Husseini, the radical leader of the Arabs in Palestine, had opposed the Palestine Mandate on the grounds that it separated Palestine from Syria; he emphasised that there was no difference between Palestinian and Syrian Arabs in national characteristics or group life. As late as May 1947, Arab representatives reminded the United Nations in a formal statement that 'Palestine was ... part of the Province of Syria.... Politically, the Arabs of Palestine were not independent in the sense of forming a separate political entity.' Ahmed Shukeiri (Shukairy) announced to the Security Council (May 31, 1956) that 'It is common knowledge that Palestine is nothing but southern Syria.'

Nevertheless, the young revolutionaries were disillusioned by the Arab states' inability to regain Palestine and came to the conclusion that the Palestinians themselves had to start harassing Israel. In fact, ever since the end of the 1948 war infiltrators had been penetrating Israeli territory to murder and rob indiscriminately. Most of them were refugees but among them were members of small secret organisations that

* *The Arab Awakening*, Hamish Hamilton, 1938.

4

were springing up in Gaza, the West Bank of the Jordan and among Palestinians in Syria and Lebanon.* Such organisations as existed were inept and careless. On the very day the Israelis occupied Gaza in 1956 they found lists of fedayeen, from the limited operations of 1954-55, in the files of abandoned Arab administrative centres. They had no difficulty in rounding up the men on the list.

Fatah, the first prominent fedayeen movement, was formed from a group of Palestinians who used to meet in the Gaza Strip after its occupation by Israel in 1956 and discuss how to combat Israel. Fatah is the reverse initials, in Arabic, for 'Movement for the Liberation of Palestine'—*Harakat al-Tahrir al-Watani al-Filistini* (*watani*=national). Fortuitously, *fatah* itself is an Arabic word meaning 'conquest'.

At its institution Fatah, according to one of its more voluble leaders, Salah Halef (Abu Ayad) 'represented a group of Palestinian youth who had revolted against existing conditions as exemplified by the divisions among Arab states, especially after Syria's secession from the United Arab Republic, and by the failure of the Arab parties to take up any struggle.'†

Yasser Arafat, underground name Abu Ammar, born in 1929 and slightly older than the others, became their 'leader'. Arafat's selection as official spokesman was a curious business. Abu Ayad described the process of selection: 'There is a

---

* There was nothing new about Arab violence against Jews in Palestine–Israel. In April 1920 in Jerusalem and May 1921 in Jaffa, Jews were murdered in outbreaks of violence. In August 1929, 133 Jews were killed and 339 injured in the religious centres of Hebron and Safad. In the 1930s organised Arab bands, encouraged by the Higher Arab Committee, raided Jewish settlements. About 80 Jews were killed and 396 wounded in 1936. In October 1938, in Tiberias, 19 men, women and children were killed. On October 15, 1938, the Jerusalem correspondent of the *New York Times* reported: 'Extremist Arab followers of the Mufti ... are rapidly achieving their aims by eliminating political opponents in Palestine who are inclined towards moderation. More than 80 per cent of the total casualties in the past few days have been inflicted by Arab terrorists on Arabs.' In retaliation, Jewish extremists attacked Arab settlements, sometimes causing scores of casualties.
† Speaking to Lutfi al-Khouli, editor-in-chief of *Al-Tali'ah*, June 1969.

special reason for choosing Abu Ammar ... that is, of us all he is the least garrulous. Actually the idea was to announce three names as the official spokesmen but they all refused. Since Abu Ammar was the only absent one, he was chosen. The decision was announced publicly and he could not but accept.'

Arafat was a shadowy figure and, understanding the value of a legend, he has fostered the aura of secrecy about his past. In fact, he is from Gaza and his real name is Abd el-Rahman Abd el-Rauf Arafat el-Qudwa el Husseini. Abd el-Rauf is his father's name, which the Arabs customarily add to the full name, and the remaining ones are his surnames. For every-day use the majority of the clan use the names el-Qudwa or Arafat el-Qudwa. Yasser Arafat has avoided mention of his full name for it reveals his kinship to the former Grand Mufti of Jerusalem, Haj Amin el-Husseini. The Husseini family lost its status in the Arab world, and if Arafat had revealed his family tree at the beginning of his career, he might have endangered his underground reputation.

In 1951 Arafat was an engineering student at Cairo University and in 1953 joined other students in carrying out irregular operations against British troops in the Suez Canal zone. As president of the Palestine Student Federation (1952-56) he became connected with the Moslem Brotherhood and when it was outlawed in 1957 as a threat to national security he fled from Egypt.

His name was certainly on the Egyptian Government's black list and he and others were prohibited from entry until 1968. Moving to Kuwait, Arafat became a building contractor, though he was ready at any time to abandon his business to further his underground activities. Tempestuous and vehement, inflexible and, at that time, ill-mannered, Arafat was a violent leader. In one incident, a new recruit rushed forwards and kissed his hand. Arafat punched him on the head, kicked him and shouted angrily, 'What are you smacking your lips for? We're all equal!'

He toured the Palestinian diaspora preaching his gospel of 'liberation' and recruiting members for his organisation. Cells were set up in Kuwait and among Arab students in West Germany, and training was started in Algeria. From 1959 the organisation's ideas were given some publicity in a 30-page monthly edited in Kuwait and printed in Beirut and entitled *Falastinuna* (*Our Palestine*).

Arafat and others like him called themselves the representatives of the 'Generation of Revenge', taking over the leadership that had slipped from the hands of the 'Generation of Disaster'. But revenge did not attract enough recruits and the limited group of middle-class intellectuals who gathered around Arafat spent their time quarrelling. The real progress was being made by powerful non-Palestinian bodies, such as the Syrian Social Nationalist Party, which was penetrating the Palestine refugee camps and other Palestinian centres, and later by vigorous pan-Arab movements. In fact, Arafat and his colleagues were operating in an atmosphere that rejected independent Palestine organisations and strove towards fusion with the dominant trends in other parts of the Arab world.

In 1959 President Nasser's office issued the slogan 'Palestinian entity', in an attempt to bring about a revival of 'Palestinism'. Nasser believed that he could awaken Palestinian nationalism and make it serve him in his inter-Arab political campaigns—those designed to make Egypt supreme in the Arab world.

Egypt even sponsored a group called the 'Organisation for Shattering Refugee Settlement Programmes' whose avowed aim was to prevent any attempt to solve the problem of refugees in the countries which had given them sanctuary.

Nasser's manoeuvre was purely political and it at once became dangerous. Nasser and General Qassem of Iraq each wanted to use the 'Palestinian entity' against the other; both wanted to arouse the million Palestinians in Jordan to undermine the Hashemite crown. Jordan fought the slogan and

Jordan's Prime Minister, Haza el-Magali, declared, '*We* are the army of Palestine; *we* are the refugees.' He and King Hussein feared that the kindling of Palestinian nationalistic feelings would endanger the state. Their fears were justified— the Prime Minister was later killed by a bomb placed in his desk drawer.

Nevertheless, King Hussein, in a speech from the throne on December 1, 1960, said: 'Without Palestine, Arabs cannot possess real freedom and genuine unity or even a good life.'

Said a commentator on Cairo Radio: 'The Arab people will pronounce the death sentence against criminal Israel, namely disappearance. Israel is the cancer, the malignant wound in the body of Arabism, for which there is no cure but eradication. There is no need to emphasise that the liquidation of Israel and the restoration of plundered Palestine Arab land are at the head of our national objectives.' (April 20, 1963; 20.55 hrs.)

'Palestinian entity' soon involved practically every Arab state—and profited none of them. Nasser had started something he could not control. Fatah exploited the confusion and the slogan, and Syria supported the movement, giving Arafat a headquarters in Damascus and providing his movement with training facilities, weapons and financial assistance.

While Arafat and Fatah were striving for power, other strong personalities were using 'Palestinian entity' and 'Death to Zionism' as levers to authority. One was Ahmed Shukeiri who was invited in September 1963 by the Arab League Council—which had its headquarters in Cairo—to 'represent Palestine' and lead a project for the revival of the 'Palestinian entity'. Shukeiri, born in Acre, was then 51, and had been Saudi Arabia's delegate to the United Nations. A fiery, fatuous demagogue, he was sacked for attacking the West too sharply without his government's authority. At the time the *New York Times* wrote: 'The UN is made up of one hundred and four nations and one Shukeiri.'

Shukeiri travelled the Arab world calling for bloody vengeance against the Israelis and working out plans for founding
the Palestinian Liberation Organisation and the Palestinian
Liberation Army. On May 22, 1964 he opened, in Jerusalem,
the first Palestinian National Congress, with a proclamation
couched in rich, ringing language: 'In the name of God, the
Magnificent, the Compassionate, Believing in the right of the
Palestine Arab people to its sacred homeland Palestine and
affirming the inevitability of battle to liberate the usurped part
of it, and its determination to bring out its effective revolutionary entity ... I do hereby proclaim the establishment of the
Palestine Liberation Organisation as a mobilising leadership
of the forces of the Palestine Arab people to wage the battle of
liberation....' Then he presented a covenant calculated to
incite the Arab mind and inspire a wish for unity. Article 5 of
the covenant stated that 'the Palestinian personality is a permanent and genuine characteristic that does not disappear. It
is transferred from father to son.' Article 13: 'The destiny of
the Arab nation and even the essence of Arab existence are
firmly tied to the destiny of the Palestine question.'

The incitement was successful but unity eluded Shukeiri.
Most of the small groups refused to be assimilated into his
organisation. Six larger organisations set up a rival union—the
Political Bureau for the Palestinian Liberation Movements—
and Fatah retained its independence.

But Shukeiri had several advantages over his rivals. The
Arab governments had committed themselves to support him
and almost all the notable figures in the Gaza Strip, Lebanon
and Kuwait had joined his organisation. Nasser apparently
assumed that the PLO was the solution to restoring his declining influence among Palestinians. He publicly recognised the
Palestine people as playing the role of 'vanguard' in the
offensive against Israel, but the vanguard would not be permitted to dictate his moves. In this he was bound to confront
Fatah. Master-minding the revolution was Fatah's declared

intention; Arafat constantly said so in *Our Palestine*. At that time few people in the Arab countries took seriously the long, tedious articles in this literary-political review.

Our Palestine called upon all Palestinians who were working within the different Arab political parties to leave these groups and work only—and directly—for the cause of 'Palestine liberation'. All Arab states and ruling parties were requested to allow the Palestinians to dedicate themselves solely to this cause and not push them into raging partisan side-issues. Many intellectual Arabs considered these injunctions presumptuous.

Those Israelis who read *Our Palestine* considered it so much chest-thumping; some of its contents seemed even more anti-Arab than anti-Jew. For instance, in August 1964 the monthly's editor, Tewfik Khuri, wrote: 'There is a well-known children's story about a group of mice who suffered from a cruel cat. The mice assembled and decided that the best way to get rid of the cat was to hang a bell on its neck, a bell that would foretell all its movements. The only problem was which one of the mice would hang the bell, and on this subject they could not agree. Today there are thirteen *cats* in the Arab league and not one of them hangs the bell on the Israeli *mouse* [my italics].'

Fatah men believed that they, the Palestinians, would have to spur the Arabs to a war with Israel. When Nasser refused to go to war and fight over Israeli appropriation of water from the Jordan, Fatah, through *Our Palestine*, called the people to revolt against the inactive Arab governments. A little later the magazine published a 'demand' to the Arab states to 'surround Palestine with a preventive belt of defences and watch the battle between us and the Zionists.'

Israel, for all the efficiency of its Intelligence Services, paid no official attention to Fatah until July 1964, when a prominent Israeli orientalist read a book called *The March on Palestine* by Naji Alush, a far-sighted Palestinian Leftist from

Lebanon. The Israeli scholar studied the chapter concerning *Our Palestine*, and perceived that behind this publication stood an organisation that recognised no restraint. He informed Israeli Intelligence so that by the time of the first fedayeen foray Israel could discern the connection between *Our Palestine* and Fatah.

Despite sharp criticism, *Our Palestine*—and therefore Fatah —preached obstinately about the need for an independent Palestinian fedayeen movement, ready to strike at Israel. Such preaching had now become an end in itself and there was talk of 'sacred violence'—a phrase lifted from the writings of Franz Fanon, a Negro psychiatrist from Martinique who had helped rouse the Algerians against the French. The Fatah men saw violence as sacred because it would not only be effective against Israel but would pave the way for a 'Palestinian national revival'.

Some Arabs cautioned that sabotage activities would simply invite massive Israeli reprisals. Naji Alush asked: 'Why should we suppose that the Israeli Army will stand with its hands tied in the face of fedayeen's attacks? The Israeli army will destroy Arab villages and cities and may even take a decisive step, and, for example, occupy the whole West Bank. ... The Journal [*Our Palestine*] considers that in the present circumstances the Arab armies are incapable of wiping out Israel, whereas it sees the Palestinian entity is capable of accomplishing this miracle. How will it be? ... Naturally the Revolutionary Road, which *Our Palestine* has chosen, is an unwarranted one, because it is built on improvisation, excitement and spontaneity. It will restore the issue to 1947 [i.e. to another defeat].'

Fatah's riposte to criticism was furious.

'We announce to the whole world that we shall launch our revolution with sticks and knives, with old revolvers and crooked hunting rifles, in order to teach a lesson to those who suffer from nightmares about Israeli tanks and planes. Everybody says that Israel will blow up Gaza, massacre the Palestinians, invade the Arab countries. Israel. Israel. Israel. But nobody considers what we can do—how we shall burn citrus plantations, demolish factories, blow up bridges, and cut off oil communication lines. The revolution will last a year, two years and more, up to twenty or thirty years. As a matter of fact, let the Zionists conquer the West Bank, blow up Gaza and massacre our population. Let the American Sixth Fleet make a move. The Arab people will stand as a dam to help the revolution. History has never witnessed the failure of a popular revolution.'

Fatah's mistake was its assumption that the revolution was 'popular'. Division and discord among the Arab states, the difficulty of obtaining recruits, the reluctance of ordinary Arabs to contribute to revolutionary funds—all this indicated a general lack of popular revolutionary spirit. Many Arabs were prepared to give oral support to war against Israel and even moral support, but Arafat and his colleagues found difficulty in bringing them to the sticking point.

Even the Saudis, who supported the fedayeen financially, did not want them too strong. If the organisations took over Jordan, then by Saudi thinking, Israel would have to move into Jordan and occupy it and Saudi Arabia would lose its buffer against danger.

Aware of their own professional military inadequacies, the Fatah leaders felt that some professional military leadership was needed and they approached Hazim al-Khalidi, a Jordanian who had served with distinction in the British Army during World War II. Khalidi, for two years commandant of the Syrian Military Academy, declined the invitation. The very professionalism which Fatah sought told al-Khalidi that Fatah had no viable military foundation. Khalidi told Arafat that he needed a secure base and that the Jordanian public must be carefully prepared for guerrilla activities before action was possible.

Despite the ten years of talking, plotting and planning the first Fatah venture was abortive. Arafat found that none of his members knew Israeli territory well enough to go on patrol to the Beit Netopha canal and plant a bomb. From Syrian Intelligence he obtained the names of Palestinians living in the Ein el-Hilweh refugee camp near Saida who had carried out 'observation missions' in Israel. He hired a small group, which was to leave on New Year's Eve, but some of the men backed out at the last moment and revealed the plan to the Lebanese security officers supervising the camp. The whole group was imprisoned but this was apparently unknown to the agents Arafat had sent around Beirut with posters announcing, 'The "Storm" troops have moved towards the occupied land to open the offensive against the enemy.' Since that time 'The Storm'—*El-Asifa* in Arabic—has been the label for Fatah's sabotage units, which, by 1972, were under Syrian control.

Other Fatah men dropped copies of 'Military Communiqué No. 1' into the letter-boxes of Lebanese newspapers, which next morning gave front-page prominence to the exploit. Two days later the Lebanese authorities leaked the news of the arrests and it became known that the Fatah claims were fabricated. It was to be the first of many false claims and exaggerations.

Fatah quickly recovered from the setback and sent the group from Jordan to the Beit Netopha canal. The Lebanese arrested Arafat and his colleagues and Arafat spent forty days in prison while an Arab-world furore raged about the Fatah operation. Egypt announced that Fatah was 'an agent of imperialism' but Dauf Ada, chief of the Baghdad branch of the Palestinian Liberation Organisation, proclaimed that it was 'the first step towards the great offensive'. Shukeiri claimed that only the Palestinian Liberation Army could authorise any Palestinian military operation and denounced Fatah for disrupting Arab unity.

The Arab press and radio in Syria, Egypt and Jordan were fulsome in their praise of fedayeen activities. *Al-Masam*, the Jordan daily, on January 19, 1965, stated: 'Groups of fighters have begun the holy war by acts of sabotage in Israel.... There is no doubt that the existence of these groups represents the aspirations of the Arab peoples, who do not believe in any other means but this of dealing with the Palestine problem.... The justification for the existence of this organisation is the exploit which we can describe in no other way but as an act of glory.'

On the same day, *Al-Gomhouria*, a Cairo daily, commented: 'Storm troops have begun to act on the conquered territory ... in order to wipe out the shame and return to us the conquered motherland.'

Akhbar Falastin, a Gaza daily, February 1, 1965, voiced the opinion that: 'The actions which have been carried out against the enemy are the natural national obligation of every Palestinian.... Acts of mining and sabotage are but one link in the chain of our struggle.'

Arafat, though seething in prison, knew what he had achieved. The abortive sabotage operation and the minor forays to follow it would be ineffective in themselves, but they would excite the Arab mind, a fertile breeding ground for intrigue. Arafat and the other fedayeen leaders subscribed to the theory that given impressive slogans revolutions generate their own forces and acquire momentum. Then, on the grand opportunity, they would become history-shaping.

Fatah and its sister organisations, none of which was yet important, needed to wait only until June 1967 for their grand opportunity in what Arafat was to call the 'war of the long breath'.

2 'To Entangle the Arab Nations'

Fatah's first subversive actions in Israel were opposed by Arab states, principally Egypt, Jordan and Lebanon. The Arab Summit meetings and the Arab Unified Command condemned subversive action against Israel for fear of the inevitable retaliation from Israel and escalation into war. Jordan and Lebanon intercepted Fatah groups attempting to penetrate Israel from their borders and sometimes arrested them. But from the first, village *mukhtars* and even Jordanian army and security officers would readily release fedayeen they had captured. In 1965 Israel made several warning raids into Jordanian areas where Fatah members had found shelter. Then Jordan acted vigorously and certain Fatah units were liquidated, while others were infiltrated by Jordanian agents. Fatah then began to use Syrian territory for jumping-off ground.

Lebanon was no more sympathetic than Jordan and its police chased Arafat and other Fatah leaders from one refuge to another, until they gave up hope of maintaining headquarters in Lebanon. Syria was the only territory left and in the middle of 1965 Arafat and his leaders moved to Damascus, though their headquarters had to be underground. From here couriers kept these key men in touch with cells abroad. Fatah was so ambitious that it was sending instructors to give secret military training to recruits in Germany. Other 'liberation' movements sprouted; most were based on small groups of acquaintances that selected an impressive title for themselves—though some were no more original than 'Black Hand' or 'Red Hand'—published a 'covenant' and soon dispersed.

During the first three months of 1965 Fatah carried out ten sabotage raids—seven across the Jordanian border, three from Gaza. The Egyptians rounded up Fatah's Gaza men and stopped them from operating. The Israelis captured some of the other fedayeen but Fatah managed to extract propaganda value from certain captives, principally from Mahmud Bakr Hijazi, a well-known petty criminal in Jordan. The organisation found ready-made publicity material in the foreign lawyers who tried to plead Hijazi's case before the Israeli court, in his hunger strikes and flamboyant behaviour in court. He became an instant Fatah hero but was soon forgotten.*

In 1965 Arafat met Che Guevara, the Cuban revolutionary, and was probably influenced by some of his ideas on 'popular wars of liberation'. If so, Guevara neither adequately briefed him nor honestly told him that the practice and philosophy of what he had done in Cuba had been a resounding failure in parts of South America. Also, for reasons to be discussed later in this book the Cuban principles did not meet Palestinian requirements.

Fatah thinkers produced a pamphlet called 'How an Armed Popular Revolution Breaks Out' and saw four basic stages:

1. The establishment of a consolidated leadership—the revolution's pioneers.
2. To win the people's confidence in the Fatah leadership, to appeal to the multitude and incite them to revenge, and to clarify the movement's objectives.
3. To plant trustworthy, indoctrinated members in all possible organisations and institutions so that there would be a

* Hijazi was exchanged on February 28, 1971 for Shmuel Rosenwasser, an Israeli watchman captured during a fedayeen raid into northern Israel in 1970.

hierarchy of command which would maintain discipline.
4. To begin the military struggle against Israel.

But Arafat and the others did not practise their own precepts; they jumped from phase one to phase four. Understandably, they did not get the following they expected when they set up, in August 1965, 'The Command of El-Asifa' (The Storm) supporters.

Already, in June 1965, Fatah delegates to the Palestinian National Congress in Cairo had met the world press for the first time and expressed their policy with a directness—'To entangle the Arab nations in a war with Israel'—which was too much for Nasser and his associates. They tried by several means to induce Fatah to dissolve itself; even Nasser's personal envoy, the respected Kamal Rifaat, was rebuffed.

By the end of 1965 Fatah had made 35 raids into Israel, 28 of them from Jordan, and nearly all against civilian targets. The Syrians encouraged the Fatah leadership to operate from Jordan in the hope that this would involve Hussein in border conflicts with Israel and weaken his standing among Palestinians living in Jordan. Also, of course, Syria could not openly be blamed for sabotage acts. Sabotage operations have no significance unless they are publicised and in 1965 Fatah operations were given little publicity. Egypt was specially mute. But the Lebanese Press Association, which had decided to ignore Fatah's pronouncements, found the organisation's theme too sensational to ignore and gave it virtually the only public exposure it received.

The group's military activities were inefficient for most of 1965 but Syrian training and improved Intelligence work made them more viable later in the year. The Arab governments, except Syria, remained anti-Fatah and in January 1966 a meeting of delegations stated: 'The irregular activities conducted by Fatah in the occupied land are ineffective. These operations cause misgivings and the Arab states must beware of them and be on the alert for any information concerning such activities.' The security services of Egypt, Jordan and Lebanon combined to work against Fatah. Largely because of this unity Fatah operations from Lebanon and Jordan ceased between November 8, 1965 and April 1966 and the only 'official' movement was from Syria.

Early in May 1966, before many people had even heard the name Fatah, Israel complained to the UN Security Council about a 'recrudescence of Fatah activity' in April—five raids in all, including three from Jordan. The Israeli delegate to the UN reported, 'The Fatah organisation publishes in the Arab press "communiqués" about its exploits. Although boastful and exaggerated, these stories are reasonably accurate about times and places.' Being reported to the Security Council was a psychological triumph but Fatah leaders were frustrated in many directions. They could not even establish themselves among the one million Palestinians on the Jordanian West Bank, although this was supposed to be the focal point from which to generate revolution. Nor did Fatah make any progress in setting up cells among the 420,000 Israeli Arabs—those Arabs who had stayed in Israel and settled down—and only about fifty of them over the years since have supplied information or provided safe houses for infiltrating Fatah agents.

In May relations between Fatah and the Syrian Government, now controlled by General Jedid, became critical because Syria wanted to control Fatah completely to make it subordinate to the Ba'ath Party. Arafat would not surrender control so the Syrians tried Fatah-type sabotage operations against Fatah. When this failed they assigned Captain Yussuf Urabi, an officer in the regular Palestinian units of the Syrian army, to take control of Fatah from inside. Urabi informed all Fatah cells that he was dismissing Arafat and taking over—but this naïve tactic exposed his intentions before he had enough power; Arafat sent his assassins who murdered Urabi in Yarmuk refugee camp. Later the Syrians named one of their own terrorist groups after Urabi.

Because of this and other sources of friction—for instance Arafat's own leading military assistant, Mohammed Mashma, was murdered—Arafat and eleven other top Fatah men were soon in a Syrian prison where they spent forty days before being released for 'lack of evidence'. But it was increasingly difficult for Fatah to operate. At the end of May 1966 *El-Asifa* published a plaintive editorial: 'In Jordan and Lebanon, the mad campaigns against the fighters of El-Asifa are intensified daily, spreading and embracing anyone suspected of fighting the Zionist invaders.... Each house suspected of giving entry to the fighters is searched, its furniture destroyed, and its inhabitants robbed....'

While harassing the Fatah leadership, Syria was nevertheless planning a terrorist war of its own. In this instance 'terrorist' is well chosen, for the President, Al-Atassi, used these words when he addressed soldiers on the Israel–Syrian front: 'We raise the slogan of the people's liberation war. We want total war with no limits, a war that will destroy the Zionist base.'

The Syrian Defence Minister, Hafiz Assad, said two days later: 'We shall never call for, nor accept peace. We shall only accept war and the restoration of the usurped land. We have resolved to drench this land with our blood, to oust the aggressors and throw you into the sea for good. We must meet as soon as possible and fight a single liberation war on the level of the whole area against Israel....' Even teachers became caught up in fiery nationalism and at a general conference of teachers on July 10, 1966 they decided 'to prepare the psychological climate for the battle of vengeance'.*

• Israel gave stern warnings about retaliation and reprisal but in fact adopted a moderate policy and did not act against Syria. This encouraged Egypt as well as Syria to think that sabotage activities could be stepped up without risk of war or massive

---

* *Documents on Palestine*, PLO Research Centre, Beirut, Vol. 1, p. 308.

retaliation. By being moderate Israel invited Egyptian–Syrian aggression. Ironically, Nasser, constantly urged to endorse terrorism, was driven into the Syrian–Fatah camp by Israeli moderation. In addition, Egypt and Syria were collaborating against Jordan, another factor working in Fatah's favour.

All this time other fedayeen groups had come and gone, their members caught by the Israelis, killed on mission or by their Syrian or Fatah rivals. But in October 1966 a stronger group emerged—the Heroes of the Return, founded by the Arab Nationalists. Its first mission was a failure—three men being killed by an Israeli border unit and the fourth captured. Based in Lebanon, the Heroes made several operations from Lebanon and Jordan. The Jordanians sent assassins to Lebanon to kill Shafik el-Hut, a member of the Heroes of the Return and head of the PLO branch in Beirut, but he escaped with only slight wounds.

The Heroes brought Shukeiri back on stage to say

'The PLO no longer consists of dreams and hopes. The PLO is now a fighting revolutionary organisation, professing action and self-sacrifice, followed by the brave fedayeen warriors.... The fedayeen will strike Israel ... they will leap forth from every hill and every *wadi*, from Aqaba in the south to Golan in the north. From now on these operations will not cease. Our heroes are prepared to open two fronts, one in Amman, the other in Tel Aviv.... Both our fields and theirs will be set on fire. There will be more than one battle. There will be a day for the Knesset, for the Hebrew University, for Natanya, Tel Aviv, and occupied Jerusalem. Blood and bullets will be the only exchange between us and the enemy.'

Such language helped to spawn new groups and late in October the Commemorative Abd el-Kader Husseini Unit signalled its inception by blowing up the Jerusalem railway near Batir. By January 1967 there were similar units—the Abd el-Latif Shararu Unit, the Ibrahim Abu-Dia Unit, the Isma'il Ben-Ibrahim Unit. All belonged to the Syrian-controlled Palestine Liberation Front.

On January 1, 1967 Fatah published a summary of its achievements with 'the destruction of dozens of tanks, the slaughter of hundreds of enemy soldiers, the creation of a dangerous, tension-filled atmosphere in Palestine....' Such grandiose claims were to haunt Fatah and other fedayeen leaders a few years later. Achievement had fallen far below expectation but in a sense Fatah *had* been successful. The sabotage operations had not so much aimed military strokes at Israel but psychological ones at the Palestinians who had to be won to the cause of revolution. Arab public opinion was dubious, for Fatah's exaggerations and fabrications were obvious, but there was some stirring among Palestinians. 'We realised,' Abu Ayad was later to say, 'that blowing up a bridge could not be a determining fact for liberation. Yet we realised that blowing up a bridge would recruit ten other people to join Fatah.'

Between January and June 1967 fedayeen groups carried out 37 operations, a significant increase on the 35 for all of 1965 and the 41 for 1966. They were well spread, too—13 from Syria, 13 from Jordan and 11 from Lebanon.*

The operations had a political and social effect on Israel—they made the Israelis more united in the face of danger. But they had no military or economic influence. Until May 1967 the casualty figures were 11 Israelis killed and 62 wounded. The fedayeen losses were even lighter in the period immediately preceding the Six-Day War—seven killed and two captured. This low figure does not so much indicate a high level of

* Fatah has claimed 300 sabotage missions before the Six-Day War. An intensive study of newspaper reports, obviously undoctored Israeli contemporary documents and Fatah's own communiqués shows this to be exaggeration. The total figure was 113.

fedayeen efficiency as—at that time—a low level of Israeli Intelligence about the organisations.

Growing restive under provocation, the Israeli Army, after a mine killed three soldiers in Judea, made a large-scale retaliatory raid in the Mount Hebron area and repulsed Jordanian army units which rushed to the scene. The raid in no way reduced sabotage but it did shake Hussein's Government and thus helped Fatah. The other Arab leaders and Fatah exploited the incident vigorously by organising sabotage in Jordan. Fatah came out of the phase with renewed prestige but was disappointed to receive no Russian praise. The only Soviet acknowledgement of the fedayeen's existence before the Six-Day War was contained in a note to the government of Israel in which the Soviet Foreign Ministry described the fedayeen as a fabrication of the Western Intelligence Services! *

* *The USSR and Arab Belligerency*, Israel Ministry of Foreign Affairs, Jerusalem, 1967, p. 37.

3 *The Rise*

Fatah credits itself with the outbreak of the 1967 Israeli–Arab War, but the Arab governments tend to dispute this, not so much because they want the credit as because naturally they want Israel to carry responsibility.* Arafat and his colleagues certainly hoped to push the Arab world into a war with Israel but it is more likely that they hoped for an outbreak in 1968-69, when they and Fatah would be more entrenched in Palestinian and Arab graces.

The fedayeen played no particular part in the Six-Day War, except that Fatah men gave covering fire to the retreating Syrian forces in the Golan Heights. The war, nevertheless, gave Fatah its great opportunity.

To appreciate the scope of this opportunity it is necessary to understand the extent of the Arab defeat. Despite an Israeli victory in 1948-49, and again in 1956, no peace terms were negotiated and tension remained high. Egypt, Jordan and Syria steadily built up their military forces, as did Israel. On May 17, 1967 President Nasser demanded and received the withdrawal of the United Nations Emergency Forces from the Gaza Strip. Five days later he closed the Gulf of Aqaba

---

* Evan M. Wilson, US Minister-Consul-General in Jerusalem at the time of the Six-Day War, says: 'It seems clear that the Arab leaders themselves were responsible for starting the June war. They had duped themselves with their own fiery rhetoric and had become prisoners of their own propaganda. They thought they would win.' *Jerusalem, Key to Peace*, Middle East Institute, Washington D.C., 1970.

to Israeli shipping. Fighting broke out on the morning of June 5, with Israel taking the initiative. Israeli planes claimed 374 enemy aircraft destroyed, mostly on the ground. Free from enemy air attacks, Israeli armoured columns entered the Gaza Strip, fanned westward into the Sinai Desert in a three-pronged advance on the Suez Canal and raced southward to Sharm el Sheikh on the Gulf of Aqaba. After only three days' fighting the Egyptian Army was in flight on all fronts. To the east, Israeli forces captured the Old City of Jerusalem on June 7, and attacked the Jordanian Army west of the Jordan River. On the same day King Hussein agreed to the cease-fire proposed by the United Nations. Egypt accepted the cease-fire on June 8 and Syria the following day, but not before losing the Golan Heights, from which so many fedayeen attacks had been made. Formal warfare ceased on June 10, but in those six days three Arab armies, though they had far outnumbered the Israeli forces, had been crushed. The Egyptian forces had suffered most of all, losing their entire air force, most of their armour and tens of thousands of prisoners.

The Arab nations were near psychological collapse and many leaders and writers were speaking freely of 'the failure of Arab civilisation'. The disgrace was immense, the sense of shame profound.* Even for Fatah the natural course would have been, after the cease-fire, to admit that the war had ended Fatah's political hopes. It had indeed, but Fatah recovered from the shock of defeat faster than any Arab nation or group, and its leaders concluded that their mistake had been in not increasing sabotage and terrorist activities. After fierce argument about ways and means, Arafat proposed that Fatah

* Dr. Yehoshafat Harkabi says that the Arab words for wrong, harm and injustice (*zulm, daym, jawr*) have a stronger connotation than their equivalents in other languages. 'It is not only a matter of iniquity but of personal injury and a sense of disgrace which cries out for vengeance.' *Arab Attitudes to Israel*, Jerusalem, 1970. Dr. Sonia Hamady, an Arab writer, describes Arab society as a 'shame society'. *Temperament and Character of the Arabs*, Twayne Bros., New York, 1960.

operational centres should be moved to the Israeli-occupied territories. Other members of the 10-man Central Committee said that this would be dangerous and impractical but Arafat won on the vote.

Fatah now gained an important psychological victory in the Arab world. The Arab armies were discredited, Nasser's prestige was low, a million Palestinians were now subject to Israeli rule. There was a vacuum. Fatah moved to fill it and planned to seize control over the occupied Palestinians and incite them against the Israelis. Collectively the fedayeen were seen as the Arab messiah. 'This movement [Fatah],' Hisham Sharabi wrote, 'was able after the 1967 defeat when despair, anguish and shame engulfed the entire Arab world from Rabat to Baghdad, to raise the banner of defiance.'*

Fatah did more than this. The fedayeen raced to grab all possible battlefield booty before the Israeli salvage squads reached it; they gained much equipment in this way. The prestige of Palestinians rose as never before; many non-Palestinian Arabs studying abroad posed as Palestinians, for to be a Palestinian was advantageous (in Arab countries and in countries sympathetic to the Arabs they were given preference in jobs, for instance) and a source of pride.† The Russians were still sceptical about the fedayeen and referred to them as the 'most backward elements' of the Arab national movement which the Chinese cultivated for their own purposes.‡

Fatah quite early defined the two main objectives for their operations along the cease-fire lines. They refer to them as 'smashing the shield'—attacks on the border towns and settlements—and 'bending the spear'—keeping the Israeli forces busy along extended front lines so as to weaken their striking

* *Palestine Guerrillas: Their Credibility and Effectiveness*, Center for Strategic and International Studies, Georgetown University, 1970. Reprinted by the Institute for Palestine Studies, Beirut, 1971.
† *Resolutions of the Palestinian Eighth National Council*, Cairo, March 1-5, 1971; published by PLO Research Centre.
‡ L. Sheidin, *'Imperialsticheskii Zagavor Na Blizhem Vostokei'*, Kommunist No. 11, July 1967.

25

force. 'We carry out two kinds of actions,' Arafat said, 'commando and guerrilla. The commandos infiltrate, perform their mission and then return to their bases. The guerrillas remain in their zones, move about, disguise themselves and attack....'*

In July 1967 Arafat infiltrated the West Bank, under the aliases of Abu Mohammed, 'the Doctor', Dr. Fauze Arafat, Dr. Husseini. His deputy, Omar Abu-Leila, 31, a graduate of Baghdad Military College, became Captain Muj'ahid. Another important person at this time was Fa'iz Khamdan, a former captain in the Jordanian army.

Arafat lived in the casbah of old Nablus in Samaria and held his meetings in small Nablus cafés or in the New Generation Library. He personally contacted almost all cells and for a man of his vulnerability was careless about security. Nablus residents recall seeing him walk openly about the streets and say that it was not particularly difficult to arrange a meeting with him. He also recruited key men for Fatah, one being Kamal Nimri, an engineer from Jerusalem. Nimri reluctantly agreed to become deputy Fatah chief in Jerusalem and like so many others was caught by the Israelis early in 1968.

Arafat had several narrow escapes from capture. Once Israeli police boarded a bus on which Arafat and Abu-Leila were travelling from Nablus to Ramallah. The fedayeen leaders were disguised as shepherds and apparently for this reason the Israelis did not ask for their identity cards. Arafat's rather distinctive features—brown, rather soft eyes, prominent nose, thin black moustache, receding chin—were not then so widely known.

Nablus was probably safe enough at that time, even allowing for the inability of most Palestinians to hold their tongues. It was a centre of extreme nationalism and it had a core of

---

*Teofilo Acosta, a Cuban journalist, in *Tricontinental*, issued by the Permanent Secretariat of the Solidarity Organisation of the Peoples of Africa, Asia and Latin America, Havana, 1968.

intelligent notables. Some doctors were willing enough to give medical treatment to Fatah men—and some of them paid for this by going to prison. Those I have interviewed say they would take the same risk again.

For Fatah, Samaria was the key region because it had many villages where cells could hide. During his six months in this region Arafat and his associates did an efficient organising job, dividing the area into sub-regions, appointing commanders, arranging dumps of arms and ammunition, starting a system of training for village youth and sending volunteers for training in Syria.

It was becoming easier to get recruits though few fedayeen volunteers were simply obeying Fatah's call for personal sacrifice. It is obvious when interviewing a score or so of fedayeen to see the influence of money, ideology, nationalism, protest, adventure, escape from personal predicaments and commitments, desire for status, relief from boredom, and disappointment, in the case of students with poor academic achievements. Fatah was successful in recruiting Palestinian students in Lebanese and Algerian colleges but its greatest accomplishment was among the thousands of Palestinian students in West Germany. Through these and other students Arafat was able to organise underground networks in countries such as Egypt and Jordan which refused him entry.

Israeli administrative methods in the occupied territory— firm and strict but humane and enlightened, with gradual relaxing of controls—influenced the great mass of Palestinians to remain neutral. They were certainly anti-Israeli occupation but they began to see that Israeli military government was much less oppressive than Jordanian 'civil' government. Nothing has more baffled and frustrated fedayeen leaders than the peacefulness of the West Bank. According to their theories a reign of terror in occupied territory was inevitable. They were sure that terror, breeding counter-terror, would alienate all strata of population and drive ever increasing numbers into

27

active resistance. They were confident that the brunt of
Israel's fury would be felt more by the Palestinians under
Israel's rule than by the guerrillas themselves. Further, they
predicted that Israel would want to conquer more territory and
to destroy the economic infrastructure of the neighbouring
Arab countries. Such a view was based on the Arab obsession
that Israel wanted an empire from the Nile to the Euphrates—
an idea that makes no military, social or economic sense.

A Fatah tactic is intimidation of anyone co-operating with
the Israeli administrators of the West Bank. After the elections
for the municipality of Jerusalem an Arab resident, Abu
Marwan, wrote an article in the Jerusalem Arab daily paper,
Al-Quds, the gist of which was: 'We oppose the annexation of
Jerusalem, but as Jerusalemites we have a stake in the way the
city is run so we should be represented on the technical committees of the municipality and every Arab representative of
those committees will start every speech by saying, "I oppose
the annexation of Jerusalem but the situation of the sewage
or schools is very bad and it should be rectified."' The same
evening Fatah radio announced, 'Whoever murders Abu
Marwan will be a martyr in the Holy War of Islam.' Marwan
replied to Fatah, in a letter published in *Al-Quds*: 'In case
you come and murder me, there are many Abu Marwans in
Jerusalem. My address is....'

With the West Bank too dangerous, the Fatah leaders
returned to the neighbouring Arab countries, leaving cells to
foment as much trouble as possible in the occupied zone.

The most efficient group to operate on the West Bank was
probably that of Abd el-Rahim Jaber, a member of the Popular
Front. He commanded in Jerusalem a group of boys formerly
associated with Fatah and another group of teenagers in
Hebron, including his younger brother who was killed while
trying to throw a grenade into an Israeli administrative building in East Jerusalem. Jaber's group was responsible for
Jerusalem's 'Night of Grenades' and for explosions in the Tel

Aviv Bus Station. When Jaber was captured—an Israeli patrol rescued him from a minefield—his second-in-command, Said Ghazawi (Abu Mansur) took over but he was killed in a skirmish in Hebron. Ghazawi would simply pick up some Arab youths, incite them with revolutionary fervour, teach them how to handle grenades and explosives, set them a target—and disappear.

Probably the most important development in 1967 was the formation, in November, of the Popular Front for the Liberation of Palestine. Then, in April 1968, the Syrians' Sa'ika (Thunderbolt) organisation made its début in the field. It was formed from the union of three Syrian–Palestinian groups, most of whose members were Ba'ath members or supporters. The Syrians supplied Sa'ika with funds, arms, training centres and propaganda. Its official leader in June 1968 was a Syrian–Palestinian officer, Colonel Taher Dablan, a dedicated foe of Fatah. Dablan lasted only six months and then, thrown out of Sa'ika, he went to Amman and formed his own organisation, the Palestinian Victory Regiments.

During 1968 the fedayeen movement became tripartite in policy. Fatah's doctrine was 'pure Palestinism', the destruction of Israel; any pan-Arab objective had no significance. The Popular Front and its factions saw the Israeli struggle as the basis of an Arab World revolution. Sa'ika and the Arab Liberation Front had no time for Palestinism and saw the terrorist movement as the means to a pan-Arab end.

4 The 'Victory' of Karamah

All three divisions of the fedayeen movement were to benefit from one of the principal events of their history—the Battle of Karamah on March 21, 1968, an action rarely given sober appraisal in the West and never by the Arabs. Karamah, a large refugee camp in the Jordan Valley, had become the main fedayeen base and Arafat had his H.Q. in the primary school for girls. His fighters controlled all services and public utilities, thus ensuring the inhabitants' co-operation.

For sound practical reasons Fatah split Karamah into nine sectors, each militarily self-contained and with reinforced bunkers. The Israelis, stung by terrorist attacks on settlements, planned to send in airborne troops and an armoured column but made the tactical mistake and, as it turned out, the strategic mistake, of announcing that the attack was imminent and of imposing a rigid advance limitation on operations. Obviously, therefore, the Israelis did not intend the action to cripple the guerrillas as a serious political or military force— as some Western observers later stated. The attack was intended as a warning to King Hussein that he should not encourage fedayeen activities.

The 1,000 Israeli troops supported by tanks and planes who made the Karamah thrust took over a strip of country 30 kilometres long by 10 kilometres wide and cleaned out Fatah bases. They gave battle to 48 Jordanian tanks, 11 artillery batteries and almost two brigades of infantry as well as 600 first-line fedayeen. The fedayeen, with such strong Jordanian support, naturally flouted a principle of irregular warfare and stayed to fight it out. They lost between 70 and 204 killed and about 130 taken prisoner. Israeli casualties were 26 dead and 70 wounded.

Military honours lay with the Israelis who destroyed enemy stores and took away great quantities, but they had seriously under-estimated the ability of fedayeen propaganda to turn defeat into 'victory' and to exploit it to the full. In a series of communiqués Fatah announced that the fighting had 'shattered the myth of Israeli air and technological superiority', that the Israeli casualty list corresponded to putting out of action about 8,000 Americans in Vietnam in a single day—on the basis of total population. This was clever sophistry, the type of tit-bit eagerly swallowed by a journalist who had to get his story in a hurry.

The pre-arranged Israeli withdrawal became a rout in the hands of Fatah's publicity men, and a few burnt-out tanks were made to look like the destruction of an entire armoured column. The Israeli 'invasion' had been stopped; the fedayeen could do what three Arab nations had failed to do. The Arab world longed for a victory and was easily convinced that Karamah was this. Abu Ayad claimed that 300 Israeli officers and men were tried for refusing to participate in the battle, a statement all Arabs wanted to believe.

For Western consumption there were stories of the many civilians killed and wounded by the Israeli strike. The Press were not so readily taken in by this: 'It was proved beyond doubt that Karamah had ceased to be a civilian settlement and had been transformed into one huge terrorist base. There were hardly any civilians in it. The civilian population had evacuated it because the presence of the saboteurs made normal civilian life impossible.'*

Dr. Hisham Sharabi was to claim that 'probably no more

* George de Carvalho, *Life*, April 5, 1968.

than 300 guerrillas', with artillery support from the Jordanian army, not only stood their ground against a superior Israeli force but inflicted heavy losses on it.

'The guerrillas burst on to the scene as a major factor in the Arab–Israeli confrontation.... Karamah was responsible for restoring Arab self-esteem and for showing the Palestinians that they not only could face the Israelis militarily but that only through armed struggle could they ever hope to defeat Zionism.... The battle marks the beginning of large scale Palestinian resistance; it was instrumental in bringing to light the existence of the Palestine Movement of National Liberation, better known as Fatah, and to cause a ground swell of pro-resistance feeling throughout the Arab world.'

However wrong he is in assessing Karamah as a fight, Sharabi correctly sees its psychological importance to the Palestinian masses. Fatah was so sure it had been victorious at Karamah that it introduced its 'Himmah' operations—actions of limited confrontation in which the fedayeen would occupy certain Israeli positions for several hours. The empty resort of Himmah was held for several hours on May 2, 1969. A similar action was fought at Sha'sha'a, and sporadic fighting occurred at Green Belt and Nahal-Golan.

Arabic acclaim for Karamah brought flocks of volunteers to fedayeen ranks and the groups were soon in competition for members by offering higher wages, more excitement, better terrorist opportunities and more authority. Competition became conflict and recruiting clashes ended in shootings and stabbings.

In an attempt to show that anti-Israel activities attracted many educated young men, Fatah in 1968 claimed the following occupational background of its members:

High school graduates	40%
Labourers and peasants	25%
Academic students	20%
Clerks and public utility workers	15%

A Beirut weekly conducted a survey of the 98 students on one of Fatah's training courses in Jordan and published a more detailed analysis.

Marital status:	92 bachelors; 6 married.
Occupation:	7 students; 23 high school students; 5 grammar school boys; 11 clerks; 6 teachers; 19 labourers; 3 peasants; 10 peddlars; 5 drivers; 4 'men of property'; 4 ex-servicemen; 1 'illiterate'.
Age:	10 aged 15-20; 75 aged 20-25; 11 aged 25-30; 2 aged 30-35.

With more manpower and better training Fatah mounted more raids—43 in August 1968 alone. But the costs were high —3·3 casualties per raid against 1·3 Israeli casualties, mostly civilian. That year the fedayeen movements collectively were responsible for 922 incidents, though many were negligible.

Fatah members were given conventional ranks—lieutenant, captain and major—and from the start there were far too many leaders for the number of rank and file. Functions were not clearly defined, thus there was great disorder. Leaders and followers did not have systematic contact but came together usually to discuss a specific operation. Many leaders and ideologists spent most of their time on ideological controversies— one of the reasons for the wide gap between leaders and the ranks.

In theory, the Military Command sent each sector commander a plan of action three months in advance. He adapted and elaborated this plan, determined the time and immediate objectives and sent orders to the group commanders, who also had considerable elasticity. In practice, as several fedayeen leaders have admitted to me, the order from the sector commander might be nothing more than: 'It's time we did something.' What was actually done depended largely on the whim, energy and opportunism of the field leader.

Fatah began 1969 with its 'Seven Points'—a manifesto of policy and intention:

1. Al Fatah, the Palestine National Liberation Movement, is the expression of the Palestinian People and of its will to free its land from Zionist colonisation in order to recover its national identity.
2. Al Fatah, the Palestine Liberation Movement, is not struggling against the Jews as an ethnic and religious community. It is struggling against Israel as the expression of colonisation based on theocratic, racist and expansionist system of Zionism and colonialism.
3. Al Fatah ... rejects any solution that does not take account of the existence of the Palestinian people and its right to dispose of itself.
4. Al Fatah ... solemnly proclaims that the final objective of its struggle is the restoration of the independent democratic state of Palestine....
5. The struggle of the Palestinian people, like that of the Vietnamese people and other peoples of Asia, Africa and Latin America is part of the historic process of the liberation of the oppressed peoples from colonialism and imperialism.

Arafat was struggling to make Fatah not only the pre-eminent fedayeen organisation but the dominant one as well and in February 1969, with Nasser's help, he became chairman of the PLO and began to reshape it as radically as he dared, planning to make it a department of Fatah, to launch joint propaganda and fund-raising activities and to supervise the Palestine Liberation Army. Wearing different hats as the Fatah

chief and PLO chief, Arafat could express diametrically
opposed views to see which one produced the better results.
Arafat's achievement in taking over PLO was a masterly if
cynical feat of political manoeuvre. He made PLO into the
'representative Palestinian body' and Fatah into the underground fighting wing of the movement.

In April 1969 PLO–Fatah established the Palestinian Armed
Struggle Command (ASC) and drew eight organisations into
it. The major non-joiner was the Popular Front. The ASC's
task was to sift and verify the military announcements of
the member groups and so obviate the absurdity and
ridicule of two or more groups claiming the same 'victory'.
Also, ASC gradually became a military co-ordinator and
planner but it failed because it had no power to *impose* planning and many times the various groups went their own way—
sometimes attacking each other by accidental confrontation
on the same mission.

All this time Arab writers and politicians were working hard
to find analogies between the Palestinians' situation and that
of other 'occupied peoples'. The Jordanian ambassador to the
United Nations, Muhammad H. El-Farra, in May 1969 could
see the Palestinian people 'facing a similar occupation, experi-
encing the same test and undergoing the same challenge which
confronted the peoples of Europe over two decades ago. They
have been subjected to Israel's policy of expansion. Palestine
resistance has precedents in many parts of the world. Do we
forget that resistance of Nazi occupation of Europe had its
headquarters in London?'*

There was also much wishful thinking. Mrs. Randa Khalidi
El-Fattal, editor of *Arab World*, expressed the belief, in May
1969, that 'by maintaining the present ration and calibre of
commando operations within the occupied territories ... the
existing atmosphere of instability in Israel may give more im-
petus to Jewish emigration from Israel and stop immigration

* *Arab World*, May 1969.

35

to it. It will eventually paralyse the economy growth of Israel ... conditions are bound to curtail foreign investment in Israel and may eventually stop it.'

But no amount of fedayeen activity or propaganda, or desperate hopes dressed as reasonable assumptions, impressed the Russians and this continued to disappoint the movement. On April 10, 1969 the Voice of El-Asifa noted: 'The greatest surprise is the stand taken by the Soviet Union. The Russians have chosen to side with the United States and Britain, even though these two powers are known to be hostile to the whole human emancipation movement. Thus, the view of the Soviet Union invites censure and raises some questions.... The Soviet Union knows perfectly well that our Palestinian Revolution is a revolution of national liberation.... That is why the Soviet Union should reverse its policy.'*

The fedayeen could at least be grateful to the Soviet for arms, for they were by now using the Russian Kalashnikov automatic rifle and Katyusha rockets.

At that period Dr. Sharabi saw the guerrillas as 'the only force totally and completely independent of Russian or American influence.' 'If the Vietnamese can fight for more than a quarter century so can the Palestinian guerrillas,' Sharabi proclaimed.† But, a specialist in such matters, he knew that the Vietnamese had natural 'safe' bases and the fedayeen did not.

Fatah communiqués were boldly phrased. 'Special group 277 has been ordered to carry out an operation of deterrence to serve as a warning to the enemy.... This morning our fighters

* Arab communists attending the July 1968 conference in Moscow were instructed to establish close contacts with the fedayeen. The collection of Intelligence was an important objective but their main task was to investigate the possibility of bringing the Palestinian organisations under their influence. It is not the organisations' extremist position towards Israel that has prevented the Soviet from officially recognising them but the realisation of the Soviet leadership that the Palestinian movement constitutes a factor of internal strife inside several Arab countries. Being aware of the problematical constitutional status of the organisations in these states Moscow practises extreme caution.

† *Arab World*, May 1969.

managed to place several high explosive charges in the Afula vegetable market.... As a result of the explosions, several cars were destroyed and it caused many casualties, dead [one man was killed] and wounded.'*

Now, a full year after the Six-Day War, fewer well-educated Palestinians were joining the movements and a French survey showed that the rank and file was predominantly of peasant and lower middle class background, with the great majority coming from refugee camps. Among 1,000 fedayeen only 8 per cent were college graduates, 32 per cent had a secondary school education, 54 per cent only a primary school education and 6 per cent were illiterate.†

Fatah and the other organisations were successful in the indoctrination of volunteers. In Jordan, Sharabi interviewed the 23-year-old leader of a Popular Front patrol in August 1969 and found him repeating his instructors' clichés. The feda'i told him

'... Only by fighting for our rights can we win them. We have learned this at considerable cost. We have also learned that our liberation—and that of the entire Arab people— can only be achieved by fighting and dying. Talk and com- promise only further degrade us.... Only the masses, the poor and the dispossessed and the revolutionary elements of the young generation are capable of rejecting compromise in favour of protracted armed struggle. Yes, in the end we shall have political settlement but not before we have liberated ourselves—from reaction as well as from Zionism and imperialism....'‡

* Voice of Fatah, Cairo, October 6, 1969. In July 1969 the Nazareth cell of the Palestine Liberation Front had put a bomb in a melon and planted it in the watermelon market in Haifa. A Haifa boy stole the melon from a vendor's booth where it had been placed and inadvertently dis- connected the detonator while trying to eat the melon.

† *Le Monde*, July 16, 1969.

‡ *Palestine Guerrillas: Their Credibility and Effectiveness*, Center for Strategic and International Studies, Georgetown University, 1970. Reprinted by the Institute for Palestine Studies, Beirut, 1971.

This young man's words should be analysed. The key phrase is *and that of the entire Arab people*. The vast majority of the Arab people are not, even by the wildest definition, subjugated by Israel or in the slightest way threatened by Israel. So what is it that the entire Arab people needs to be liberated from? Imperialism has long since disappeared from the Middle East, so presumably 'reaction' is the people's enemy. And this must mean reactionary Arab governments. It would seem then that Sharabi's interviewee was fighting Israel only indirectly; his real enemy was the Arab Establishment.

At the end of 1969 El-Asifa broadcast this message:

'Our fighters have learned to land blows on enemy targets and to return from battle with very few losses. Despite this progress some men still believe that the words "fedayeen activity" means certain death, and that anyone going out to fight is as good as dead. Men who think that way can be divided into two categories: Those who have failed to understand the progress of the revolution. They are prepared to join noncombatant units, thereby giving the warriors their moral support. Those who fear death and do not know that death is better than refugee life. Our answer to those who have opposed us, claiming that our losses are many, is that the number of fallen among refugees in the camps due to poverty and natural disasters far exceeds the number of terrorist casualties.'

With 2,567 missions* attempted in 1969 heavy casualties were inevitable, though the figure per encounter (2·4) was lower than in 1968. This was the peak period of terrorism and organisations sprouted by the score. Many assumed pretentious titles, published manifestoes and military announcements and then faded away. But at least these groups were honest in intention. Many rogues and swindlers set up 'resistance' groups

* It is not possible to analyse the scope and effectiveness of these missions but many—the Israelis would say the majority—consisted of firing across the cease-fire lines.

and induced wealthy Arabs to contribute to their funds. To give their collections an air of authenticity they issued official-looking receipts which at least allowed a merchant to save face when he knew that he was being swindled. Sometimes the swindling was at the point of a gun.

Military training in Fatah and the other organisations has been of uneven quality. Fatah could afford to give its early members only ten days' instruction in weapon handling and sabotage techniques. Most instructors were officers and non-commissioned officers from the Arab regular armies, seconded to the fedayeen groups more to keep an eye on them than from a real desire to see them become efficient.

After the fight at Karamah, when hundreds of volunteers joined Fatah, too few instructors were available and Fatah used any man who knew how to handle weapons and instruct in fieldcraft heedless of whether he had had a 'proper political education' or was genuinely revolutionary in outlook. Some training was crude, new recruits were often roughly treated and physical punishment was commonplace. Desertion became rife. Sharabi says that as many as 50 per cent of the deaths incurred during the post-Karamah period occurred in training, often as a result of inadequate medical facilities.

At the end of 1969 Fatah had about 20,000 members, half of them members of the military arm. In addition was the Popular Militia—several thousand armed youths from the refugee camps. By mid-1972 Fatah's strength was down to about 4,000, many of them men unable to find more gainful employment.

By summer 1969 training was more efficient. Punishment was discarded and Chinese-trained instructors brought in the Chinese system of self-criticism. Also, political education was stepped up to as much as ten hours a week; every camp had a small library on revolutionary theory and guerrilla warfare. By 1970 volunteers were getting several months' infantry and commando training. Since then those who are considered to show promise are sent to officers' or specialists' schools in Egypt, Algeria, Syria, Libya, Iraq, China, North Vietnam and, lately, Cuba.

Fatah fedayeen have been gaining probably their most valuable experience in the camp set up for them by former Algerian guerrillas in the coastal hills west of Algiers. They have been taught how to get through 'impenetrable' barriers, by experts who often broke through the one built by the French along the Tunisian border in the late 1950s. Arafat prizes these fedayeen and hopes to use them to breach Israel's Jordan Valley security fence—when he regains control of Jordan.

Most physical training exercises are carried out to '*Wahad, itnein, fedayeen*'—'One, two, fedayeen'. Shouting is a feature of nearly all training. The observer cannot be sure if the shouting is designed to impress the foreign visitor (it usually does); to frighten the Israelis (who consider it ridiculous); or to overcome lack of confidence (which it probably reflects). No doubt it also creates a sense of solidarity.

The Popular Front's training programme at its height had a heavier political bias than that of Fatah, with emphasis on the establishment of cadres capable of running bases, forming and giving purpose to clandestine cells and planning sabotage action. The usual course, first in Jordan and later in Lebanon, lasted 18 to 20 weeks. After the split which gave birth to the Popular Democratic Front the movement lacked cadres; there were students of politics who knew nothing of military matters and fighters without political education. Political education was based on the writing and careers of Politzer, Marx, Engels, Lenin and Stalin, with many lectures on the development of revolutions and the defeat of imperialism. The Popular Front has always claimed that its military training is tougher than Fatah and this has largely been true because the Front has lacked the financial resources of Fatah.*

* PFLP men were said to live on cockroaches and snakes during 100-mile endurance marches.

Most weapons used by fedayeen were Soviet- or Chinese-made. The principal cross-border weapons were Katyusha rocket-launchers and 60-mm and 120-mm mortars, some of them French. Most light machine guns were Russian-made, but the heavier machine guns Chinese. I have seen jeep-mounted recoil-less and other light guns. Most ammunition comes from Egypt, Syria and Algeria and some from the European black market. Explosives are plentifully stockpiled and in 1972 were being supplied principally from Libya and Algeria.

5 *Popular Front*

It is interesting to speculate on the outcome of the fedayeen war had it been left to Fatah to wage without the dubious assistance of the other groups. It seems just possible that over a long period Fatah could have achieved some of its aims. Certainly the world image of Palestinian resistance would have been better. The other groups, with their more extreme policies, destroyed world sympathy.

Chief of these groups is the Popular Front for the Liberation of Palestine, PFLP, whose leader is George Habash. Habash was born in 1926 in Lydda (Lod) to a Greek-Orthodox corn-dealer and spent most of his early years in Jerusalem, where, during the Mandate, he was troublesome to the British. He studied medicine at the American University in Beirut, 1944-51, then married and fathered two daughters. Habash was organising and leading an underground Palestinian move-ment—the Arab Nationalist Movement—spreading from Aden to Damascus and from Tunis to Baghdad, long before Arafat was active as a leader.

Habash and the Arab Nationalists, like Nasser, opposed Fatah's terrorist tactics but were themselves drawn into sabotage activities and in 1966 they founded their own terror group—the Heroes of the Return. After the Six-Day War, while all Arab movements were painfully re-assessing them-selves, Habash and his colleagues abandoned the Arab bourgeoisie and turned their activities to the working class.

42

The Nationalists proclaimed themselves to be a Marxist–
Leninist movement and were inspired, they said, by the 'freedom fighters' of China, Cuba and Vietnam. Habash saw the
terrorist movement not only as the forerunner of a struggle
against Israel but the nucleus of a profound social revolution
in the entire Arab world. And for this revolution to be
effective Anglo-American interests in the Arab world had to
be fought.

Habash then brought the Popular Front into being to
operate as the extreme left of the terrorist movement. Also,
just after the Six-Day War, Habash founded the Youth of
Revenge. By December 1967 the Heroes of the Return, the
Youth of Revenge and Ahmed Jibril's Palestinian Liberation
Front were amalgamated into the PFLP to counteract Fatah's
growing power. Habash and his assistants launched a powerful
propaganda campaign against it. This choice of priorities—
anti-Fatah rather than anti-Israel—might seem irrational; it
need only be explained on the ground that Israel is a means to
an end, not an end in itself.

The Popular Front's over-riding objectives were these: to
dramatise internationally the plight of the Palestinians and
their determination to try to force the world to return them
to Palestine; to show the rest of the Palestine movement that
desperate measures would work; and to show Arabs and other
governments that the fedayeen would have no part in a settlement with Israel that did not regain Palestine as an Arab
land. Only by 'Vietnamising' the Arab situation, the PFLP
spokesmen insisted, could there be hope for successfully can-
celling out Israel's technological superiority and American aid.

Habash had no chance of winning the fight with Fatah for
it was a cohesive organisation while his was fragmented. He
was arrested in Damascus and imprisoned. Jibril supported
the Syrians and in October 1968 he expelled the Youth of
Revenge from the Popular Front, though on what authority
is doubtful. The Heroes of the Return, in sympathy, joined

the Youth of the Revenge and retaliated by sacking Jibril. So two Popular Fronts now existed, but Jibril quickly named his group the General Command of the Popular Front. More fragmenting followed; some of Jibril's chief colleagues left him to form the Organisation of Arab Palestine.

Habash escaped from prison in November 1968 and returned to his headquarters in Amman to find a rebellion on his hands. Two of his chief assistants, Nayef Hawatmeh and Salah Rafat, had accused the absent Habash of being a 'fascist demagogue' and wanted all bourgeois removed from key positions. Habash thugs beat up Hawatmeh men in the refugee camps and then small but bloody fights occurred in Amman suburbs.

The conflict reached such a degree of bitterness in April 1969 that Hawatmeh published a pamphlet accusing Habash's 'gang' of the murder of two members of his group, Muhamed Ibrahim Khalifa and Mundhir Abd Latif Al Kadari. The pamphlet's language was forceful. 'The Popular Front is slaying revolutionary fighters in the streets of Amman and in fascist prisons. . . . Habash is trying to tear the resistance movement into pieces from the inside. . . . This fascist gang is sabotaging the security of the resistance movement and is opening the way for counter-revolutionary forces to intervene in order to destroy the resistance movement.'

Hawatmeh and his colleagues alleged that Popular Front men seized Khalifa with two others on April 15 and barbarously tortured him because he was one of the principal Hawatmeh men in the Amman camp. Then they threw him into the street; he died soon after. 'He did not fall as a victim of Israeli Intelligence or by the bullets of conquest,' the pamphlet notes, 'but by the hands of a gang of the Popular Front which daily is turning more and more into a fascist front, including gangs of rascals and ruffians having no trace of patriotic sentiment.' Al Kadari was shot to death in a street in Amman.

After these and other acts the Popular Democratic Front for the Liberation of Palestine—as Hawatmeh's group was now known—called a conference of the leaders of the armed struggle organisations, national bodies, trade unions, the Communist Party, the Lawyers' Association, the Doctors' Association and many other groups. This conference announced that it 'condemned the fascist methods, stained in blood, adopted by the Popular Front.' After that, Hawatmeh's group campaigned continually against the excesses of the Popular Front. His PDFLP quickly absorbed the Palestine Revolutionary Left League and the Popular Organisation for the Liberation of Palestine. Hawatmeh co-operated with Fatah until December 1969 when he quarrelled with Arafat as well —and another split developed.

Against this background of intrigue, violence and extremism it is easier to understand the operations of PFLP, whose actions sometimes seem to be designed to embarrass Arab governments rather than Israel. 'Operation 707'—the hijacking of an El Al aircraft from Rome to Algeria in July 1968—is an example. The Algerians wanted no part in the plot and are still convinced that the PFLP hijackers were incited by Egypt, which wanted to embarrass President Boumedienne. Another anti-Arab operation was the blowing up by PFLP saboteurs of the Tapline, the oil pipeline carrying Saudi Arabian oil to the Mediterranean. Saudi Arabian papers savagely attacked the PFLP 'which operates at the service of the devil'.

Habash's theory has always been that to kill a Jew far from the battlefield had more effect than killing a hundred Jews in battle. 'When we set fire to a store in London [referring to the incendiary bombs in Marks and Spencers, August 17, 1969] those few flames are worth the burning down of two kibbutzim, because we force people to ask what is going on....'*

* To Oriana Fallaci, an Italian journalist, reporting for *Life*, June 22, 1970.

But PFLP was prepared to kill Jews anywhere, as at Hadassah Hospital, Jerusalem, where bombs placed near the oxygen reserve killed and injured a number of Israelis and caused fires on February 16, 1970. Five days later PFLP members planted a bomb in a Jerusalem supermarket, killing two people and injuring nine. An Arab Anglican clergyman was implicated in the supermarket explosion though he did nothing more than pass money. He and another Arab clergyman spent some time in prison. When the Anglican Archbishop in Jerusalem, the Very Reverend George Appleton, visited them for the first time he found them very frightened. 'They were doing nothing against their conscience,' he said, 'politics were more important to them than their religion. If the fedayeen become important again these men would return to the movement; they would need to do so for their own safety.' Archbishop Appleton believes that Christian fedayeen were more ruthless than Moslem fedayeen, once they decided to take action. Habash, it has been noted, is a Christian, as is Nayef Hawatmeh.

The Habash group has killed or injured many non-Jews, too. A PFLP terrorist threw grenades into the El Al offices in Athens, November 27, 1969, killing a Greek child and injuring 15 people. Greek reaction was forthright.

> 'The new criminal action ... does not constitute an act of war, but is a cowardly act of callous criminals. The Greek people have a long and glorious military history, but all of their military struggles for national rights or cultural values are distinguished by the element of valour, and especially by respect for ... any society not at war. The carrying out of such despicable murderous activities in neutral territories, under guise of supposed military action, proves an absolute lack of spirit of self-sacrifice for a just struggle, as well as cowardice.'*

* Greek Deputy Premier in *Bulletin*, Athens News Agency, December 1, 1969.

On February 12, 1970 PFLP terrorists attacked an El Al plane at Kloten airport, Switzerland, killing a pilot. On February 21 other PFLP men planted a bomb in a Swiss airliner which blew up in flight to Israel, killing the crew and passengers—55 lives. This crime caused world revulsion. A Bangkok newspaper commented: 'One's sympathies must go to the victims of the attack and their relatives. But they ought to be extended to the Palestinians whose cause has all but been ruined by the Zurich incident.... The guerrillas' attacks on aircraft affect the course of the war only in ways detrimental to them....'

In May that year PFLP fedayeen crossed 500 yards into Israel and prepared an ambush. They allowed a military patrol to pass. 'Then came a target more to their taste—a bright yellow school bus on its customary morning run, packed with five- to eight-year-olds from a moshav [co-operative farm] called Avivim.'* When the bus slowed for a turn in the road the Arabs attacked. At point-blank range, scarcely 20 yards, the fedayeen fired by remote control three 82-mm bazooka shells. The driver, two teachers and seven children died instantly; another student and teacher died later and the remaining 20 aboard the bus were wounded.

Apparently the PFLP did not see this operation as an atrocity, for they quickly claimed 'credit' for it, and were not worried by world reaction, typified by a US publication: 'If there is anything like a lunatic, radical fringe in the Palestinian resistance movement it is this splinter group—the PFLP—which has openly admitted responsibility for the most recent atrocity in the Holy Land ... and so, once again, the Arabs have succeeded in demonstrating that they can be their own worst enemies.'†

PFLP also succeeded in demonstrating that Israel would exact a heavy price for attacks on El Al aircraft. On

* *Time*, June 1, 1970.
† *America*, June 6, 1970.

December 26, 1968 terrorists attacked a plane at Athens airport, killing one civilian and wounding another. Reprisal was swift and decisive: two days later the Israelis sent helicopter-borne commandos to Beirut where they blew up 13 Arab passenger planes, without loss of life.

Habash is always ready to justify PFLP tactics and told Oriana Fallaci that in war it was fair to strike the enemy wherever he happens to be, and that this rule led PFLP to the European airfields where El Al planes land or take off. Miss Fallaci pointed out that the planes carried citizens of neutral countries. Habash's answer:

'The non-Israeli passengers are on their way to Israel. Since we have no control over the land that was stolen from us and called Israel, it is right that whoever goes to Israel should ask for our permission.... We want a war like the war in Vietnam. We want a Vietnam war not just in Palestine but throughout the Arab world.... Our struggle has barely begun, the worst is yet to come. And it is right for Europe and America to be warned now that there will be no peace until there is justice for Palestine.... The prospect of triggering a third world war doesn't bother us. The world has been using us and has forgotten us. It is time they realised we exist, it is time they stopped exploiting us. Whatever the price, we'll continue our struggle.... To harass, to upset, to work on the nerves through unexpected small damages.... This is a thinking man's game.... The only way to destroy the enemy is to give a little blow here, a little blow there; to advance step by step, inch by inch, for years, for decades, with determination, doggedness and patience. And we will continue our present strategy. It's a smart one, you see; would you really want to fly El Al?'

Habash told Miss Fallaci that the worst obstacles have always been those placed by Arab reactionaries, 'Like Saudi

Arabia, where the majority of oil wells are in American hands. Or Lebanon, with its rotten government. Then there is Jordan, whose king is ready to recognise Israel. . . . We are the joker in the deck. Without our consent the other Arabs can do nothing, and we will never agree to a peaceful settlement. If the Arab countries think they can gang up and make peace over our heads they are mistaken. All we have to do is to assert our power in one country and the rest will lose their resolve and start backsliding.'

In June 1970 Habash claimed that PFLP was responsible for 85 per cent of the military activity inside Israel, about 50 per cent of operations in the occupied territory and virtually all the incidents in Gaza. But PFLP has not engaged in military activity in the accepted sense, though its fedayeen have been given some military training in ill-equipped camps. Their daily ration, in mid-1970, was mostly boiled beans, with possibly meat once a week. Most free time was taken up with study of Marxist and Leninist classics. A little later PFLP founded a marine section, some of whose members have been caught smuggling weapons and explosives into Israel.

Finance has been more difficult for PFLP than for Fatah because Habash and his colleagues would not accept money from 'reactionary sources'—meaning Saudi Arabia and Kuwait. 'If the financial problem becomes crucial we will take money away from those who have it,' he said. 'We will take it, not ask for it. Those who join the Popular Front know that we aren't joking. It is us who give the revolutionary momentum to Palestine, not Fatah. The real people, the proletarian masses, follow our lead.'

Aggressive immoderation led PFLP into the mass hijacking of September 1970, the act which precipitated the so-called civil war in Jordan. For Christmas that year the organisation, as if thumbing its nose at the world, put on sale a special series of season greeting cards for the holidays—in the form of five flight tickets of the airlines they had attacked in September.

Fedayeen

After the crushing of the fedayeen in Jordan PFLP was quickly in operation, planting a bomb in Tel Aviv bus station on November 6, 1970. The Lebanese newspaper *Al-Amal* congratulated the fedayeen on its success. 'The explosions in the very heart of Tel Aviv have put the resistance on the path of effectiveness. *If one ignores the human aspects* [my italics], the striking of any strategical target in the very country of the enemy is a legitimate act, as the objective of the resistance is to strike at Israel's heart. The battlefield is unlimited.... Now, after the operation in Tel Aviv, faith in the resistance, its methods, effectiveness and goals has been restored.'

Israeli counter-measures and general lack of Arab popular support inhibited PFLP actions during 1971 but it claimed credit for the attack on the tanker *Coral Sea*, 78,000 tons, near the Straits of Bab el Mandeb in June. A speedboat fired ten bazooka shells at the tanker, causing some damage. The attack was intended to deter oil exporters from using the Israeli Red Sea port of Eilat.

The group developed a new terror tactic in December 1971 by sending parcel bombs to addresses in Israel, mainly from Austria. Disguised as boxes of chocolate, books and desk diaries the parcels were designed to explode on opening. Israel had developed an instrument which 'smells' explosives and it was used to detect parcel bombs; there was one casualty in Israel—a police engineer.

Habash, conscious of having said too much in the past, was now saying little and leaving the talking principally to Ghassan Kanafani, 35, a sensitive novelist but an insensitive revolutionary who was killed in Beirut on July 8, 1972 by a bomb booby-trapped in his car. Kanafani saw everything in terms of the relentless march of history rather than in immediate humanitarian terms. He told me, in January 1972: 'Black September [the war in Jordan] was logical. There should be no sentimentality about it. There could be ten Black Septembers. Fatah is too sentimental but that is not our way. The revolution is only in the pre-revolution stages and the few hundred Palestinians dedicated to revolution are the catalyst which will produce the Arab revolution. There is much more to it than anti-Zionism. There must be social and cultural revolutions and the Arab world must confront the United States.'

Kanafani believed that Gaza was the key to fedayeen activity, with cells in the Strip from which fedayeen activities could radiate. He insisted that any ebb and flow of terrorist activity in Gaza was the result of orders from Beirut and that Israeli military and police activity had no bearing. 'When the Israelis issued each soldier with a plastic ladder to reach rooftops quickly we were pleased. This proved we hold the initiative in Gaza.' Like most Arab intellectuals, Kanafani produced figurative analogies. 'We are one strand of string which will make a strong bridge.' He likened the heroism of the 'defenders of Gaza' to those in Stalingrad or any other city besieged in World War II and was exasperated that others could not see it this way.

To Kanafani, prepared to manipulate endlessly, the conflict with Israel was a way of life. Reverses depressed him personally but his ideology and dedication were impervious to them. Completely uncompromising, he had more of a pathological hatred for the Jews than most fedayeen leaders have. Because it was Kanafani who announced PFLP's role in the Lod airport massacre some Palestinians believed that the Israelis killed him in revenge. The BBC correspondent in Beirut reported that a PFLP splinter group could have been responsible.*

A serious splintering occurred early in 1972, this time with

---

* I liked Kanafani personally and had joked with him about some prominent souvenirs in his office—the coats of arms of the American Embassy in Amman and of the Jordanian Embassy in Beirut, both stolen as souvenirs during riots. Marxist, Che Guevara and Mao posters adorned the walls and mortar bombs were holding down papers on the shelves. 'We're stupidly sentimental about life,' Kanafani told me on that occasion.

the formation of the Popular Revolutionary Front for the Liberation of Palestine. This dissident faction accuses the Habash group of being 'rightist'. Even within the remaining part of the PFLP there is division. The Rightist group, led by Wadi Haddad, Ahmed Khaled and Mohammed Mussalami, favours hijacking as technically and strategically advanced; the left, led by Abu Shehab, Abu Khaled and Abu Ali, considers the idea anarchic and of no consequence to Israel. The right wants appeasement with the Arab states and a new deal in relations with Egypt while the left considers that contact should be with Arab national liberation movements and not with governments.

Habash, at the centre though previously closely associated with the right, has faced many problems in trying to reconcile the two. His frustration was evident in his comment at a Press conference in March 1972: 'The terrorist movement is declining: total impotence has come over the Arab bourgeois régimes and the reaction of this impotence is seen in a hostile attitude towards the resistance movement.'

Despite its brief and bloody history PFLP says in its credo: 'Because our struggle is a just struggle we are confident that we can win the support of all progressive and peace-loving peoples of the world....'

But internal peace has eluded the PFLP. Bassam Abou Sharif, who succeeded Kanafani at the age of 29, was injured and blinded by a parcel bomb explosion. Then somebody sent him poisoned sweets. As Kanafani had told me, 'Life tends to be precarious for some of us.'

6 *The Fedayeen in Jordan*

As early as January 1966 King Hussein had seen the danger of fedayeen activities and on January 5 he attacked the PLO for its 'treasonable' attempt to undermine Jordanian unity and to create a separate army. On June 14, after several incidents in Jordan, Hussein again denounced PLO leaders and their supporters for 'their subservience to international communism' and said that all hope of co-operation with PLO had vanished. In return Shukeiri made it clear that Jordan was the principal PLO 'liberation' target.

Commenting late in 1966 on the infiltration of Syrian saboteurs via Jordan into Israel, the king said: 'These so-called commando activities are contrary to what was agreed on at Arab summit conferences but for quite a while there has been a new trend—to direct these activities against us even more than against the Israelis. We have captured shipments of arms coming into Jordanian territory and people have crossed over the border to create trouble here ... to spread the idea of assassination ... to create chaos wherever and whenever possible.'* In view of the positive and oft-stated views by both king and fedayeen leaders it is rather surprising that both sides seemed prepared to ignore the danger of war between them.

Before the Six-Day War King Hussein fought Fatah and the other organisations toughly and intelligently. His efficient

* *US News and World Report*, December 26, 1966.

53

Intelligence Service gave him the information which his Bedouin soldiers acted on. But war fever brought some sort of reconciliation and terrorist prisoners were released under the influence of the unity the war had induced. The fedayeen now assumed they had a right to use Jordan as they wished, without any reference to Jordan's king or government.

The Jordanian Government and Fatah embarked on the liberation of Palestine but with such different policies that conflict was incessant and two separate states grew up on the East Bank—the Hashemite Kingdom and the Palestinian Fedayeen State. In many ways Arafat seemed to rule Jordan, or at least to be the co-ruler.

Hussein has been widely criticised for allowing the fedayeen too free a hand at a time when he could easily have clamped down on them. The explanation is simple. Hussein—and Arafat—believed that a Palestinian State was about to be created on the West Bank. Neither of them wanted this to happen—Hussein because it would mean the loss of a principal part of his kingdom, Arafat because it would mean, as he saw it, the end of the 'Palestine problem' and therefore the end of Arafat. Both men panicked. Arafat rushed to promote an 'armed popular revolt'; Hussein needed Fatah to bring the West Bank to a state of political frenzy where no statehood would be possible. So, while no public reconciliation was proclaimed—indeed, outwardly, Hussein and Arafat continued to be enemies—there was a union of intention.

A four-man team of scholars sent to the Middle East by the 'American Professors for Peace in the Middle East' organisation from June to July 1968, found to their surprise that the 'fedayeen problem' was much more dangerous than the 'Arab–Israeli problem'. The professors were startled to discover, for instance, that faculty members of the University of Amman were among the most active recruiters for fedayeen units and that some of them were officers in these units. The Americans had a private meeting with a group known as

'Intellectuals of the Commandos' who stated that resistance organisation was so strong in Jordan it could assume power any time it wished. The purpose of the fedayeen was to foment another war as soon as possible, which they believed could be brought about by forcing Israel to such extensive retaliation that the other Arab states would initiate a new war against Israel or that the internal disruption of life in Israel by fedayeen raids of increasing severity would force Israel into a preventive war. If another war began soon it might take one of two directions. Either Israel would occupy even larger portions of Arab territory which provide a source for an even larger underground army for national liberation, thereby causing Israel to choke from its increased Arab population; or a new war would escalate into a world conflict in which case the Soviet would see to it that Israel was destroyed no matter what happened.*

Fatah and PFLP rapidly established bases, training and supply centres along the whole central Jordan Valley. So completely did the terrorists control the East Bank of the Jordan that tens of thousands of peaceful farmers fled. Scores of thrusts across the border invited return fire from the Israelis. Jordanian attempts at controlling the fedayeen were hesitant. South of the Dead Sea a Jordanian unit encircled a Fatah group and ordered it to leave within 48 hours. The Fatah leader refused to accept the ultimatum and said that even if the Jordanians fired first he would not reply. Before the situation could be tested the Bedouin officer had orders from Amman to withdraw.

This double approach in the field merely reflected the differences between Hussein's words and actions. In September 1968 he said, 'It would be an unparalleled crime if anyone were to dispatch fedayeen to carry out operations that would supply the enemy with a cause for oppressing our brothers in the occupied territories. Such activities would only advance

* *The Arabs Need and Want Peace, But—*, APPME, New York, 1968.

the success of Israel's plans for curbing the power of the resistance.... It is my duty to oppose such a plan.' But while he was saying this his army officers were advising terrorists how to cross the Jordan and later these army officers supplied covering fire against the Israeli army.

On November 4 and 5, 1968, there was an open and serious clash between Jordanian Bedouin troops and fedayeen when three camps were shelled; several men were killed and arms and food depots damaged. The 'criminal terrorist group' which came under the heaviest fire was identified as elements of the PFLP's extremist section. Hussein and Arafat came to terms: Hussein agreed to the guerrillas maintaining training camps in the Salt Valley, Jerash and Kerak while the fedayeen agreed to 'disappear' from Amman's public view. The agreement left many Jordanians intensely irritated by the trouble Palestinians continued to bring to the country. The settled communities of Salt, Jerash and Kerak were particularly annoyed.

Fatah was so confident at this time that in a broadcast from Cairo it announced: 'The Palestine organisations are alone competent to punish those Palestinians who deviate from the revolutionary line and we reject controls [i.e. imposed by Arab states].... Arab frontiers must remain open for our operations and we demand immediate liberation of Palestinian revolutionaries detained in Arab prisons. The insecurity of Palestinian fighters inside Arab frontiers cannot continue and we cannot guarantee to remain quiet in the future. We shall not pay the price of a peaceful settlement....'

Such an aggressive stance apparently cowed the king, for at the beginning of 1969 he submitted: 'I would not exercise control or try to limit fedayeen activity emanating from Jordanian territory. The fedayeen constitute the fighting element of the Palestinian nation.'* He was trying at the time to bring Bedouins from the East Bank and refugee Palestinians from the West Bank into what he called 'Jordanian family' to

* *Sunday Times*, January 19, 1969.

counter the urging of General Qassem of Iraq that a Palestinian republic be established in the West Bank and Gaza Strip.

But no unity existed among the groups of Palestinians in Jordan because they came from very different backgrounds. There were the well-established and prosperous pre-1967 Palestinians, the pre-1967 refugees in camps, the post-1967 refugees and the fedayeen Palestinians. Anxious to show his tolerance and support for the fedayeen movement, Hussein included a Fatah man, Nazim Zarou, in his government—that of Bahjet al-Talhuni—as Minister of Municipal and Rural Affairs. This desperate expedient probably amused Arafat; he was so determined to avoid an all-out open confrontation with Hussein until he *knew* he could win, that before mid-1970 he and his senior aides defused dangerous situations which had developed between the Jordanians and extremist terrorist groups. Militarily, Fatah steadily entrenched itself in Amman, Irbid, Salt and Zerga. In June Hussein moved his troops against the fedayeen to drive them out of his capital. During the bloody fighting fedayeen seized a number of American hostages and killed a US military attaché, Major R. J. Perry, with a burst of automatic fire through the locked front door of his home.

The Popular Front occupied two Amman hotels and held as hostages the 32 American, British and West German guests. Habash brought them together at the Intercontinental Hotel and, on June 12, made a speech in which he said, 'Our code of morals is our revolution. What saves our revolution, what helps our revolution, what protects our revolution, is very right and very honourable and very noble and very beautiful.... We were fully determined, that in case they [the Jordanian Army] smashed us in the camps we would blow this building and the Philadelphia all over.... You are not better than our people....'*

* From a rare pamphlet produced by PFLP Information Department, *Our Code of Morals is Our Revolution*, 1970.

Habash wrested concessions from Hussein by threatening to blow up the Intercontinental Hotel. The PFLP was then able to measure the international effect of such blackmail. It professed to see no other way of challenging the great industrial powers which proposed to determine the Palestinians' fate without consulting them.

To emphasise the fedayeen supremacy Arafat forced Hussein to include several pro-fedayeen politicians in his government. Arafat was now signing correspondence as 'Commander-in-chief of the Palestine Revolution'. This left the king humiliated and angry while his army sweltered in its own anger. Hussein's officers referred openly to the fedayeen as terrorists. Mostly of Bedouin origin, they chafed under many humiliations, often being stopped by Palestinian militiamen in the streets, searched and questioned. Terrorist effrontery was so bold that in Karamah the fedayeen prevented Jordanian Crown Prince Hassan from entering their base, and when General Kailani turned up with an escort the terrorists threw them out, telling Kailani he was lucky they were not obeying their orders to shoot him.

Wasfi el-Tel, the most able Prime Minister Hussein ever had before 1972, suggested that the king turn Jordan into a fedayeen state, proclaim himself its leader and control the terrorists by forming them into a type of militia. Such a display of initiative, Tel stressed, would give Hussein the public backing he needed to his authority over Arafat. But the king rejected the idea.

Israeli counterblows might have given Hussein some respite had he exploited them. But the fedayeen, though retreating from the Jordan valley into the big refugee camps, became even more arrogant. Fatah instituted 'courts' to try West Bank visitors accused of spying; they executed several such 'spies'. At roadblocks they extracted 'fees' and 'donations' from businessmen. They would accept no instructions from army or civil police and they embarked on intensive recruiting and propaganda campaigns, the latter aimed especially at the Bedouin on whom Hussein most strongly relied. It was efficient propaganda, for some Jordanian Arab Legion officers joined the fedayeen, and tribal leaders promised support. Arafat's line was that anybody living in Jordan was a Palestinian and therefore 'entitled' to a share in the fruits of the popular revolution.

With Hussein still indecisive, men such as his uncle, Sharif Nasser Ibn-Jamil, and General Kailani formed organisations ostensibly to fight the Israelis but in fact to sabotage the fedayeen structure. They were fairly effective but the powerful Fatah propaganda machine was quick to counter any move by Hussein and his government. Armed clashes became increasingly frequent yet in his speeches Hussein identified himself with the saboteurs.

Other fedayeen leaders differed from Arafat on matters of policy. Subhi Yassin (later assassinated) of the Vanguard of Self Sacrifice wanted a Palestinian republic on Jordan's East Bank; Habash wanted a showdown with Hussein; Hawatmeh urged Arafat to take a stand against the Jordanian bourgeoisie. Indeed, the bourgeoisie were making a lot of money by selling supplies to the terrorists.

At this time few journalists bothered to call at the Jordanian Information Ministry; they got their accreditation and press passes from offices run by various fedayeen groups. These offices provided everything—communiqués, press conferences, private interviews with authorised spokesmen. Fatah had a reception team of 25 educated fedayeen to meet and guide visiting newspapermen. Specially selected journalists were given the privilege of some 'genuine action'. Fatah took a Scandinavian TV crew to the 'Jordan River' and allowed them to film a fedayeen patrol crossing 'under fire from the Israelis'. In fact, the river was the Yabok; the Israelis were other fedayeen and they were careful where they fired their bullets.

Tension mounted rapidly and a crisis occurred in September 1970 when Jordan followed Egypt in accepting the Americaninitiated cease-fire, agreeing to the resumption of peace talks under Dr. Jarring. The protesting fedayeen went on the rampage and the Jordanian army organised a campaign to curb Fatah and its allies. Shortly before the appointment of a military government in Amman, special units, with the collaboration of leading East Jordanian groups in Maan, Kerak, Tafileh, Shobak, Russaifa and other parts of south Jordan, mounted a wide operation to eliminate fedayeen from these areas. It was so successful that virtually no fedayeen remained. The 'civil war' was an extension of this conflict.

At this critical point PFLP put into effect the plans evolved since July by Habash and his principal lieutenant Wadi Haddad, to hijack several foreign aircraft—planes owned by Swissair, BOAC, TWA, Pan American and El Al. Habash was in North Korea but the operations were successful except in the case of El Al. On the Israeli plane the male hijacker was killed and his accomplice, Leila Khaled, was imprisoned. The Pan American plane was flown to Cairo, where it was blown up. The others were forced to fly to Dawson Field, near Amman, where PFLP used them and their 300 passengers as hostages for political blackmail, forcing Britain, Germany and Switzerland to give up terrorists held by those countries, including Leila Khaled. But they failed to blackmail the Israelis. The fedayeen had sworn they would extract hundreds of heroes of the Palestine Resistance from Israeli gaols in exchange for hostages trapped by the hijackings. They got nothing.

Aircraft worth nearly £12,000,000 went up in flames—and all because of the exasperation of the militant fedayeen on the airfield. PFLP's leaders had not wanted to destroy the planes, needing them for further bargaining. But the militants thought this was weakness. It was typical of the gulf between the intellectuals in Beirut and the fedayeen in the field who saw everything in black and white.

'The hijacking of those airliners is the shame of the Arab

world,' Hussein told a journalist from *Le Figaro*. 'Things cannot go on as they are at present. Every day Jordan is sinking a little farther. The commandos must respect the agreement made with the government or take the consequences. What is at stake is the unity of Jordan, her position in the world and that of the army.' The position was even more critical than the king stated. Jordan's very sovereignty and Hussein himself were at stake, for while the hijacking negotiations were in progress fedayeen in north Jordan had established what they called the 'first Arab soviet', in Irbid, the country's second largest city. The inevitable war broke out, the hijackings acting as the catalyst which brought on the test of strength between the royal troops and the fedayeen. Hussein told Wasfi el-Tel to break the organisations, generally by isolating various groups and crushing them one at a time.

The fedayeen leaders' entire strategy of defence was based on what they called 'the supporting Arab front', that is they counted on the intervention of the masses in the battles. Arafat believed that when the Jordanian tanks entered Amman thousands of ordinary Palestinian people would come into the streets to demonstrate and to serve as a living wedge between his men and the army, which would never dare to shoot down civilians. Perhaps he had never read Nasser's dictum: 'One tank is enough to disperse thousands of demonstrators.' The living wedge did not materialise.

One fact is particularly important. The struggle was neither waged along Palestinian versus Jordanian lines nor on the basis of nationality affiliation, but rather according to political inclination and, to some extent, according to social standing. Most of the Palestinian community remained neutral and some supported the government. Significantly the Jordanian units that shelled the refugee camps around Amman were composed mainly of soldiers of Palestinian origin. Arafat had counted on these Palestinians turning against their Jordanian leaders.

Hussein had 60,000 men under arms, including 2,000 in

the air force, which had eighteen Starfighter Interceptor air-craft and twenty Hawker Hunters. The army's two armoured brigades were its strength, for the tanks and armoured cars were Bedouin-manned and utterly loyal to the king. He could implicitly trust 25,000 of his troops but had doubts at that time of the loyalty of the rest; these doubts were soon dispelled.

The opposing Palestine Liberation Army, most of its units based in Syria, had a paper strength of 10,000, Fatah had 15,000, the PFLP and others 5,000; in addition there were the thousands of 'militia' or fedayeen irregulars who had taken over the streets of Amman and other cities. In controlling the towns of Ramtha and Irbid, just south of the Syrian border, the fedayeen dominated the border crossings so that they could receive reinforcements from Syria. Hussein ordered Brigadier Ghasid to send tanks into Ramtha to secure the vital road to Syria, but the attack failed. Ghasid withdrew his tanks to the south and west and thus permitted fedayeen reinforcements to pour in from Syria. Nevertheless the Jordanian Army was dealing brutally with fedayeen in Amman, and Arafat was about to announce his acceptance of a truce. Over Voice of Palestine radio, Arafat said emotionally, 'Thousands of people are under the debris of Amman.... Hunger and thirst are killing our remaining women, children and old men. It is a massacre never before seen in history. A sea of blood and 25,000 killed and injured of our people separate us from the Jordan Government.'*

The fedayeen radio in Damascus broke down but, according to the authoritative Egyptian newspaper *Al-Ahram*, the Iraqi Government fed false information to the fedayeen Baghdad radio to the effect that Arafat had rejected the truce. 'In this

* The true casualty figures will never be known. Soon after the September 1970 fighting Arafat repeated that 25,000 Palestinians had been killed or wounded, but early in 1972 he gave this figure for a seven-year period. Hisham Sharabi told me that he estimated casualties at about 14,000. Robert Regulary of the *Daily Star*, Toronto, who has researched the problem, puts the figure at between 6,000 and 8,000. An Israeli source quotes 3,000 killed.

shameful situation,' *Al-Ahram* said, 'the Iraqi Government had no other purpose than escalation.'

As Arafat received better information about the fighting he was glad he had not agreed to a truce. Hussein held very few towns, only the Saudis supported him and if the Kuwaitis and Libyans held to their decision to suspend his annual grant his nation's economy would be ruined. The Syrians could easily intervene from the north and the Iraqis from Mafraq; defeat would then be inevitable. Hussein's troops fought fiercely and Field Marshal Majali offered a reward of £5,000 for the capture of George Habash and Nayef Hawatmeh.

On September 23 Hussein proposed a four-point plan which would have left Arafat with bases in Jordan. At first the fedayeen leader rejected it—a decision which led to the deaths of many more of his followers. But on September 25 he accepted a cease-fire arrangement. On Damascus fedayeen radio he announced: 'Our great people, our brave revolutionaries, to avoid more innocent bloodshed and so that the citizens may care for their wounded and get the necessities of life, I ... agree to a cease-fire and ask my brothers to observe it provided the other side does so.' But in some places shooting did not stop for some days.

Under violent criticism from most Arab governments, Hussein justified his attack on the fedayeen.

'We have reached the point where my people living in Jerusalem under foreign military occupation [the Israelis] were ten times more secure in their homes than people living in Amman, our capital. No Israeli on a kibbutz has one millionth of the trouble we have had here.... When people see the amount of arms and ammunition the guerrillas had in Amman, and the preparations they made for fighting here, they may well ask, how did we allow things to reach this pass. I can only answer that after the June war—the June disaster—I was so concerned with rebuilding the army, with the recovery of our lost territory.... They [the guerrillas] talked about resisting Israel but it was not a question of Israel at all. It was a question of takeover here. I was always puzzled by what they meant by "Palestine revolution". I could understand very well "Palestinian resistance" but not "Palestine revolution". We could not separate those who were genuine fedayeen from those who were extensions of political movements in the Arab world.... Here was a resistance, or what was supposed to be one, doing its utmost to destroy the respect and support of its own people.... I brought in a government which they practically chose [the Rifai Government dismissed by the king the night before the fighting began] and a chief of staff [General Mashur Hadithi] who had some connections with them, in a last attempt to bring some sense to the situation. But our problems increased. There was not a single unit in the army or air force that had not been provoked, in terms of their families and homes molested.'*

The king told other correspondents that he had been misled by his Intelligence Service about the strength of the fedayeen and the extent to which they had penetrated Jordanian institutions; an odd 'excuse' considering the efficiency of that organisation. His chauffeur was a terrorist and his cook had important fedayeen connections. His soldiers had found 'real underground cities stuffed full of arms' and in these bases all kinds of foreign experts, including Chinese ones.†

General Numeiry, President of the Sudan, led a peace mission to Jordan and returned to Cairo to report on the 'mercilessness' of the Jordanian Army. 'We left Amman with the one impression that there was an overall plot for the annihilation of the brave Palestinian Resistance. The Jordanian authorities have a pre-arranged conspiracy to crush the Palestinian people, and

* Murray Sayle, *Sunday Times*, September 27, 1970.
† Jean-François Chauvel, *Le Figaro*, October 15, 1970.

they will go on deceiving and eluding until they have carried out their conspiracy.' The president did not report that Arafat had told him that the fedayeen would go on fighting no matter what agreement was reached. They controlled the whole of northern Jordan, Arafat had said, and they were capable of launching a guerrilla war. Fatah could 'resist and resist' for a long time.

Hawatmeh was one of the first to rationalise the defeat, deciding that it was 'essentially a mistake to confront the régime in conventional warfare. . . . The battle is not yet over, we have not been wiped out. And we will not be wiped out as long as there are men to bear arms. The task of liberating Palestine requires a firm national base. Because of the distribution of the Palestinian people Amman is the logical candidate for that base. Two-thirds of the people of Jordan are Palestinian. Amman is the Hanoi of the Palestinian revolution.'*

Predictably, Red China blamed 'US imperialism' for inciting Hussein to act against the fedayeen. 'The reactionary atrocity on the part of the Jordanian military government was wholly engineered by US imperialism. Developing and growing in strength the Palestinian guerrillas have increasingly become a serious obstacle to US imperialist aggression in control of the Middle East. With bitter hatred for and mortal fear of the Palestinian guerrillas, US imperialism has been racking its brain in wildly scheming to stamp out the raging flames. . . .'

An agreement between Hussein and Arafat temporarily put out the flames. Hussein, still trying to lead the hounds but show sympathy for the hare, broadcast to his people:

'The heroism of the army and the sacrifices of the compatriots transformed steadfastness into an epic. Out of the call for steadfastness and for struggle the fida'i action was born to Jordan, Palestine and the entire Arab nation. This was an honourable and valiant birth to which all our hearts turned with confidence, love and hope. Jordan viewed the

* *An-Nahar*, Beirut, October 10, 1970.

fida'i action as a part of itself, a mainstay of its steadfastness and its strong arm in the struggle. Jordan is fida'i action itself. If the Jordanian people are the fathers of the army, they are equally the fathers of the fida'i action.... With God's grace, the first fruit of co-operation, understanding and faith came in the form of the agreement with the Palestine Liberation Organization Chairman, brother Yasser Arafat. This agreement reinforces the firm foundations of our noble people's unity. It consecrates the sacred cohesion of the Jordanian armed forces and the fida'i action.... We shall not tolerate anyone forsaking or disregarding this action at any time.... I refuse to criticise or slander the fida'i action in any way.... I have avoided slander all my life because this is my character and these are my ethical values. I consider the fida'i action dearer than myself and Jordan. I shall not let the fida'i action be slandered by anyone....'*

Despite the agreements, sporadic fighting between army and terrorists continued and there were vociferous denunciations of the Jordanian régime from Iraq and Libya and from terrorist groups. Arab leaders from Sudan and Egypt appealed to King Hussein to stop 'liquidating' fedayeen groups in Jordan. To one such appeal from the Rector of Cairo's Islamic Al-Azhar University, Dr. Muhamad al-Faham, Hussein replied: 'I say with grief in my heart that a group of people from whom God had withheld His guidance and who had lost their way, falsely claimed to be carrying out fida'i action and thus harmed honest fida'i action and its reputation.... By God, we care more about fida'i action than those who are shedding crocodile tears over it. Fida'i action is for us and from us.'†

But Hussein's protestations meant nothing to Habash: 'The Jordanian régime used the battle to create an abyss between

* Amman Radio, October 14, 1970, quoted from BBC Monitoring Service.
† Amman Radio, March 30, 1971, quoted from BBC Monitoring Service.

the Palestinian and Jordanian peoples so as to crystallise a social force on which it could rely in attacking the resistance.'*

Having had time to digest the lessons of the war, Arafat summed it up in June 1971: 'Rebelliousness had taken over from revolution. Our movement had been laid down in the refugee camps for 20 years and when the opportunity came to fight back our freedom of action inevitably led to demonstrative and defiant behaviour which angered the Jordanians. With unified planning and co-ordinated military action there'll be no more mistakes.'† But Habash's analysis was more accurate than Arafat's, for there had been more mistakes and Hussein had already acted.

The last substantial fedayeen units left Jerash, Irbid and Amman, under army pressure, in April 1971. Then about 2,000 dug themselves into bunkers and tunnels in the wooded hill country west of Jerash. In May and June 1971 Hussein's army again went on the offensive, shelling fedayeen bases near Jeralt and Salt and intercepting patrols heading for the Jordan. In June Fatah claimed that Hussein was deliberately making the fedayeen the target of attacks by Israel. Hussein's ruthlessness and determination was largely brought about by his discovery that the new Algerian Ambassador in Beirut, Mohamed Yazid, was trying to help organise the Palestinians and that Algerian deliveries of arms had arrived for the fedayeen.

The end came in July 1971. The Jordanian army moved against the fedayeen in their tunnels and bunkers, though Amman communiqués said that the army was simply having 'manoeuvres with live ammunition'. There was shellfire and heavy machine gun fire and although the fedayeen fought back with mortars and with night counter-attacks they were driven from their major positions. The battle was brief and bloody. About 200 fedayeen were killed and 200 evaded the dragnet,

---

* In a memo to the PLO Central Committee, published in *Al-Hadaf*, December 26, 1970.
† Derek Maitland, *Toronto Star*, June 25, 1971.

most of these splashing across the Jordan to surrender to the Israelis. The Jordanians took 2,300 prisoners; of these 1,550 were disarmed and allowed to return to their homes in Jordan, Syria, Iraq and other Arab countries. They were judged to be 'good' fedayeen—mostly Fatah men—who would not again fight Hussein. The 750 who remained under arrest were 'bad' fedayeen, members of PFLP.

A *New York Times* reporter who observed the action noted (July 18, 1971): 'It was clear that the guerrilla movement was entering another phase of its long and tumultuous decline.... As usual at times of commando defeat some Palestinians said hopefully that now, at long last, adversity might force the guerrillas to unite.... The commandos are a spent force spurned by more and more of the Arab world.... Arabs do not admire losers.'

The fedayeen left in the country after the July fighting were bottled up in the thin bare valleys running westward towards the Jordan, vulnerable to the Jordanian army and therefore easier to control. They are more vulnerable, too, to Israeli air strikes. This final conflict contributed to the fedayeen decline as an Arab political force and made nonsense of the Palestine National Council's meeting, held in Cairo a few days later; the Council quickly wound up its business without having achieved unity among the represented organisations. It also showed how support had waned in Arab capitals. In September 1970 the Syrians had moved tanks into Jordan in support of the fedayeen; in July 1971 Damascus did no more than send a five-man military 'study group'.

Even in Jordan many Palestinians showed a new coolness towards the fedayeen movement; to all those who favoured a peaceful settlement with Israel the fedayeen collapse in Jordan seemed to offer hope that the overall Middle East situation might grow more stable. The headman of a Jordanian village that had suffered from terrorist presence was interviewed by a German television team. He complained that: 'These bugs had come not to liberate Palestine, but to destroy Jordan.'*

The Jordanian victory over the Palestinians strengthened the Jordanian identification; Palestinians living there were much more 'Jordanised' and Jordan clearly became a politically institutionalised entity, while 'Palestine' was shown to be an idea, a confused community, and factious organisations.

Any possibility of the fedayeen re-establishing themselves in Jordan was destroyed by an announcement on Amman Radio on August 18, 1971: 'We completely reject not only what is put forward by the guerrilla organisations which have taken over the Palestine Liberation Organisation and the Palestine National Council but any dialogue with those organisations, which represent nobody but themselves. They have become a fifth column.... If the immature mentality of these organisations led them to imagine that the Jordanian working paper [suggesting a formula by Arab co-operation] submitted to the envoys of the Saudi king and Egyptian president is addressed to them, then these organisations are still up to their ears in delusion....'

But the delusion is obsessive. The Voice of Fatah on August 25, 1971 broadcast a statement issued by the Jordanian National Front, a fedayeen organisation which pledged itself to make Jordan once again a safe base for the Palestine revolution. Some observers believed that the fedayeen movement could have made itself popular in Jordan. 'The guerrillas blew it. They could have set up a model system and got the people's support. Instead they were brusque and arrogant. They were convinced that all revolutions succeed inevitably. A Western diplomat said: "At the lower level they were pure souls whose cause was just. But their leadership was splintered. Fatah is run by a bunch of idiots!" '†

The 'civil war' in its several phases was the fedayeen movement's first real military confrontation and at least it proved

* West German Television Second Network, July 7, 1971.
† Robert Regulary, *Daily Star*, Toronto, 1972.

to the leaders that the rule that irregular forces should not stand and fight must be obeyed. The defeat damaged Arafat's prestige as a military commander and, more importantly, it opened the way for the Maoists and Trotskyists to gain more control within the fedayeen movement. The extremists' hands had been strengthened and in Cairo on November 28, 1971 an extremist group assassinated Wasfi el-Tel, that rare figure, an Arab political realist and the principal architect of the fedayeen downfall in Jordan. This was a desperate act and it reflected the depth of fedayeen frustration over Jordan. In February 1972 a terrorist, at Brunn, near Bonn, West Germany, shot and killed five Jordanians as 'traitors'—a multi-murder concealed with singular skill by the German police, perhaps because they did not catch the murderer.

Wasfi el-Tel would no doubt have been happy to see Israel disappear in an earthquake but he also preferred some form of co-existence to unending hostilities and lost wars. As a realist, his firm aim was stability in Jordan and in an attempt to achieve it he co-operated in Israel's 'summer visitors scheme'. Under this plan the Jordan bridges were opened and Arabs were freely allowed into Israel and the occupied West Bank to trade and to visit relations. No formalities were required though Israel reserved the right to refuse entry, a right rarely exercised. Arab visitors were also allowed to leave without hindrance. In 1971 112,000 Arabs visited the Israeli-controlled territories and in 1972 the figure was expected to be 150,000. In the summer of 1972 many foreign tourists also crossed the Jordan bridges. To the fedayeen, Tel's co-operation in the scheme to bring about some degree of peaceful co-existence was more of a crime than his crushing of their movements.

Many minor incidents have occurred within Jordan, but here few fedayeen have escaped. Fedayeen leadership is content to keep the Jordanian pot simmering with what amounts to suicide missions until it can be brought to the boil.

7 *The Lebanese Dilemma*

The fedayeen movement was established in Lebanon long before the 1970 crisis in Jordan. Beirut was a much more convenient political centre than Amman and the large camps of Palestinians provided recruits for the growing fedayeen forces. If Amman was the field centre for the organisations Beirut was the intellectual centre. The fedayeen and their supporters found the climate more pleasant, communications with the rest of the world better developed and the Lebanese more easily manipulated. But the arrangement suited the fedayeen much better than it did the unhappy Lebanese, who at best have been inconvenienced by the Palestinian presence and at worst physically attacked. In some ways the Palestinian–Lebanese relationship has been more extraordinary than the Palestinian–Jordanian association.

Towards the end of 1968 Fatah, Sa'ika and PFLP began to build new bases on the western slopes of Mount Hermon, near the converging borders of Israel, Syria and Lebanon. This is a wild, thinly populated region of ravines, forests and caves and the fedayeen were well entrenched before the Lebanese Government knew the extent of the menace. The army tried to keep the fedayeen east of the Hasbani River and to limit their numbers by economic blockade. Both policies failed.

The Prime Minister, Abdullah el-Yafi, announced 'There are no fedayeen in Lebanon' and went on repeating it. In this he was using a well-worn Arab tactic: by refusing to admit the existence of a crisis it does not exist and there is no need to deal with it.* Yafi was certainly in a difficult situation. If he sent his army against Fatah he would make the Lebanese Moslem population hostile; if he openly helped Fatah he would anger the powerful Christian faction which opposed the presence of fedayeen on Lebanese territory. An all-out conflict could cause mutiny because the officers of the Lebanese army are mostly Christian and the rank and file Moslem.

Yafi was also worried about the certainty of Israeli reprisals if the fedayeen became too troublesome so he and Arafat decided on a fine balance of terrorist activity; enough to disturb the Israelis but not enough to make them strike into Lebanon—a move which would agitate the United States and France, the defenders of Lebanon.

The fine balance did not survive the PFLP attack on the El Al airliner in Athens and the consequent Israeli commando raid on Beirut airport also brought down the Yafi Government. In the turmoil Fatah brought more terrorists into the Hermon area and infiltrated others into the big refugee camps in the coastal region, including Ein el-Hilweh. This led to clashes with the Lebanese army and about twenty demonstrators became casualties. Fatah failed in the subsequent bargaining to win authority to use Lebanon as a springboard for attacks on Israel.

Late in 1969 the army encircled terrorist units near Majdal Silim, captured most of them and shot those who tried to break through. Fatah retaliated by seizing several Lebanese border posts and this sparked incidents in several parts of Lebanon—but the civil rising Fatah hoped for did not occur. In fact, along the border many Moslem groups turned against the fedayeen because they feared a destructive civil war.

---

* 'Arabs sometimes tend to downgrade reality, giving greater importance to words.... Language for Arabs is not a means to describe reality, it is reality itself.' H. E. Tutsch, *Time Bomb in the Middle East*, Friendship Press, New York, 1971.

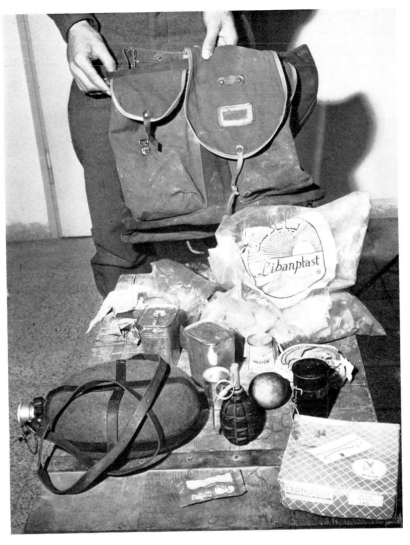

The fedayeen of 1965 had primitive equipment. This is the
kit of a feda'i sent on a sabotage mission in 1971

Above left: A trainee feda'i faces a daunting leap during
combat training while an officer shouts encouragement.
Training camps like this exist in Lebanon, Syria, Libya and
Algeria   *Photograph: Yousuf ben Mokrid*

Palestinian women in training under officers of the Palestine
Liberation Army—a regular military formation. The purpose
of this training is to inspire spiritual involvement in the
cause rather than to make the girls into combat soldiers

Fedayeen in an ambush position in the desert cliffs. Many have been killed on such missions, for there is no avenue of escape

Above right: A fedayeen patrol, photographed by a PLO cameraman, leaving Lebanon for Israeli territory

The wreckage of an Israeli school bus after an attack near the northern border. Fedayeen fired a katyusha rocket by remote control. Most of the children travelling in the bus were killed

Following the decline of fedayeen influence Israelis and Palestinian Arabs have been able to work together in many fields and as members of the same labour unions. Here Arab and Israeli are working in a metal factory.

A copy of a painting which was included in an exhibition in an Arab girls' school at Khan Yunis. It purports to show how Israelis attack Arab women

Nevertheless, subsequent publicity has aimed at producing the impression that the Lebanese had actually risen in revolt in support of the Palestinians. The expensive wall calendar for 1972 published by PFLP includes a picture of street fighting with the caption: 'The Lebanese revolt in solidarity with the resistance.' The rioters were, in fact, Palestinian students from the four Beirut universities. Several are identifiable in the picture.

After much friction the Lebanese and the fedayeen reached agreement in Cairo. The fedayeen came out of the negotiations rather well. They took over policing and control of all fourteen refugee camps in Lebanon, where leaders were given official permission to make uncensored speeches. The government agreed to give the fedayeen certain well-defined areas for occupation and to surrender all fedayeen prisoners. The fedayeen movements gave practically nothing in return, beyond promising not to parade the streets of Beirut in full military gear and to surrender the occupied border villages, which they did not need anyway.

Like Hussein in Jordan, the new Lebanese premier, Saeb Salam, wanted to appear, for the sake of Arab world relations as well as for local peace, friendly to Arafat. After an hour-long meeting with Arafat, Salam was asked his impression of the PLO chairman and Fatah spokesman. Salam was fulsome: 'It is the impression of a friend who meets a brother fighter embodying the Palestine-Arab campaign. Arafat has been an old brother and friend, even before the formation of the Resistance. My house is his house, for he is a dear brother. Lebanon, too, is his home in his capacity as representative of the brother fighters and of Arab Palestine. On this occasion, I wish to say that we will continue to co-operate with our Palestinian brothers ... to promote their campaign—a campaign which we strongly support—and to preserve Lebanon's interests, for which they care as much as we do.'*

* Beirut Radio, October 24, 1970, quoted from BBC Monitoring Service.

Unfortunately, this was not true. While the fedayeen might be heroes to the Palestinians living in refugee camps in southern Lebanon they were hoodlums to the Lebanese civilians who feared and detested them. Reports of brutality were—and still are—commonplace in the Beirut press. One of the worst crimes occurred on the night of November 15, 1970 in the small town of Aitarun, in southern Lebanon, when fifteen terrorists surrounded the house of Mahmoud Faiz Murad. Three of the terrorists tried to take Murad away by force but he, his father and his wife, in her ninth month of pregnancy, resisted. The terrorists shot and killed all three Lebanese on the spot.*

A village notable, Ali Hassan, told a Lebanese reporter: 'We probably made a mistake when we were drawn into the current of emotion and allowed the terrorists to enter our village. Had we refused, our village would have remained unaffected. But we received them and gave them all necessary aid and assistance. The result was that they forgot all about Israel and proceeded to liquidate us.'

In June 1972 a Lebanese villager, Ali Makna, heard that his two teenage sisters had a taxi ride with a Palestinian whose fedayeen name was Abu Hamido. As a matter of family honour, Makna shot the girls dead in their sleep. This started a right-wing campaign to rid the country of the fedayeen. Leaders of the predominantly Christian Phalangist Party demanded an end to the 1969 Cairo agreement providing a Lebanese sanctuary for the organisations. The men of Ali Makna's village armed themselves and paraded the streets calling for an end to fedayeen activity in Lebanon. To avert the crisis a PFLP 'revolutionary court' sentenced Abu Hamido to death: he was driven handcuffed to the place of execution but the village elders argued that to kill him was contrary to their religion and morality and he was reprieved. The PFLP still wanted to 'liquidate' him as an example to those who might 'seek to harm or undermine the prestige of the revolu-

* *Al-Hayat*, Beirut, November 17, 1970.

tion'. But too much harm had already been done. Many girls have been abducted and their families still do not know what has happened to them. It is presumed that willingly or unwillingly they live in the refugee camps. Others have been raped and some then murdered.

Disturbing incidents proliferated, largely because the fedayeen considered they were a law unto themselves with the same rights in Lebanon that they had claimed in Jordan. On New Year's Eve, 1971, Palestinian and Lebanese fedayeen attacked a Lebanese police post and patrol near the Syrian border, killing a policeman and wounding another. The incident further strained relations between Lebanon and the terrorist organisations and with Syria. The Lebanese press condemned the attack and one paper said 'The Palestine commandos must act like saints to be accepted in Lebanon.'*

Perhaps in an attempt to show goodwill to Lebanon, a week later Fatah produced a Palestinian who had supposedly been hired by Jordanian Intelligence to blow up a car near Sabra camp, which held many fedayeen; the plan, Fatah spokesmen said, was intended to disrupt relations between Lebanon and the Palestinian organisations. But in the same month fedayeen showed their displeasure with anti-terrorist Lebanese by bombing the offices of the newspaper, *Lisan al-Hal*, and a pharmacy belonging to an outspoken opponent, Pierre J'mayyel.

Despite total control over the great sprawling Palestinian settlements, Fatah and the others have failed to revolutionise the great bulk of the Palestinians and to impose a political structure.

But the fedayeen, however ineffective, are likely to remain an irritant in Lebanon for a long time. Egypt has an interest in their presence there and in their stirring up trouble on the Israeli border. It is Egypt's policy to sponsor anything which keeps the Middle East on the Security Council agenda and shows that the region is still a threat to world peace.

* *Daily Star*, Beirut, January 5, 1972.

Fedayeen

As for the Lebanese Government, it will allow the fedayeen to use Lebanon as long as they remain ineffectual.* Deciding on the degree of ineffectuality provides the Lebanese Government with its most sensitive problem, for its estimate of how far the fedayeen may be permitted to go differs from that of the Israelis. Inevitably, the growing 'Jordanisation' of Lebanon and increasing fedayeen activities along the border have provoked Israeli reaction. In May 1970 Israeli units killed forty terrorists in the Hermon sector and demolished fifteen small Fatah bases. They conquered Jebel Russ, which gave them visual and tactical control over the area previously used by fedayeen for shelling Israeli settlements. For a long time Israeli patrols made daily sweeps inside the Lebanese border. The Israelis made another raid on January 15, 1971, this time sending in troops by sea and air, to attack fedayeen bases in the coastal town of Sarrafand, 40 miles south of Beirut.

In 1972 fedayeen hit-and-run operations became too frequent for the Israelis. They were particularly incensed when, in February, terrorists ambushed an Israeli engineer and decapitated him, then killed a man and his wife, and three soldiers. The Israeli army made a three-day incursion reprisal into Lebanon, again demonstrating its intention to ignore the frontier when operating against fedayeen gangs. An interesting sidelight was that the Security Council condemned Israel for its aggression but deleted from its resolution a paragraph which 'deplored all actions which have resulted in the loss of innocent lives'. This meant, in effect, condemning the Israeli incursion but condoning the earlier fedayeen raids.

Late in June 1972 it was evident that reprisal and warning attacks would become more severe. On June 19 two Israeli civilians in a bus were injured and two soldiers wounded by a landmine. Israeli planes promptly attacked fedayeen targets

* The opinion of Mrs. Walid Khalidi (wife of Professor Khalidi), principal member of the Arab Women's Information Committee and director of the Institute for Palestine Studies. She is also sister of the Lebanese premier.

ten miles north of the border, scoring direct hits on a concentration of fedayeen in Hasbaya. On the central part of the front, near Ramiyeh, Israeli troops captured five high-ranking officers of the Syrian regular army. This was a significant capture and it gave substance to the Israeli claim that Syria and Lebanon were making joint military plans against Israel.

The Lebanese premier again called in Arafat who promised that the fedayeen would 'freeze' their attacks on Israel; Salem pointed out that the previous promise had been kept for only four months. From Cairo, President Sadat suggested a solution —that the fedayeen organisations go underground. This did not appeal to Arafat for in going underground he would be in danger of being forgotten by the people he claimed to represent. It was, in any case, a non-solution as only strong organisations escaping a powerful government go underground; to go underground in Lebanon would achieve nothing for the fedayeen.

Lebanon was again caught in the middle of the conflict after the murder of eleven Israeli athletes at the Olympic Games in Munich on September 5, 1972. Three days later waves of Israeli jets attacked ten targets in Lebanon and Syria, and penetrated as far as the Mahr el Bared camp north of Tripoli, which is used as a training centre for Fatah's youth wing. Casualties may have amounted to 300 and inevitably some people who were not fedayeen were killed. A few days later the Israeli Army made a 36-hour raid into Lebanon to blow up houses and other buildings used as fedayeen bases, and once again to warn the Lebanese Government of their dangerous position. The result was that the Lebanese Government set up military checkpoints throughout southern Lebanon to prevent fedayeen entering the area; also, they were forbidden to carry arms outside their own camps. Salam and Arafat met seven times in seven days in efforts to reach a compromise, but any agreement could last only until the following fedayeen action across the Israeli border.

Fedayeen

The most dangerous threat to Lebanese security is the existence in Beirut of the headquarters of so many fedayeen organisations. The Sabena hijacking, the Lod airport shooting and the Munich massacre were masterminded from Beirut. The Israelis are unlikely to allow the fedayeen leaders unlimited latitude in using Lebanon as a refuge.

Fedayeen organisations proliferate in Beirut, have a brief independent existence and are then taken over by the larger groups. By 1972 veteran newspapermen in Beirut had given up trying to sort out the complexities of group affiliations and membership. Each organisation has been infiltrated by agents of each other organisation and by agents of Arab governments. Every major decision of Fatah, every transfer of personnel, is known in Cairo, Damascus, Tripoli and Baghdad within hours. Arab communists have established their own organisation, Al Ansar, to penetrate the Palestinian movement and create a new centre of gravity inside. Since July 1971 Communist influence has increased. Such is the confusion that officials at the two large propaganda and information offices—the PLO Research Centre and the Institute of Palestinian Studies—do not know where various groups and offices are to be found.

Yet another factor first came into play in 1972 with the formation of the clandestine 'Support Lebanon' group to campaign for the fedayeen to leave Lebanon. In August Ahmed al-Fakhri, a leader of the Syrian-supported Sa'ika organisation, was killed in Lebanon in mysterious circumstances. He was said to have died in a car accident while patrolling an area in east Lebanon, but perhaps not coincidentally his death came after a series of assassination attempts against senior fedayeen leaders by 'Support Lebanon' agents.

With so much pressure against them in Lebanon it is not surprising that during 1972 the fedayeen planners moved their principal arsenal as well as some camps into Syria where government support for the movements is stronger than in Lebanon.

President Assad said, in September 1972, that far from curbing fedayeen activity in the face of Israeli reprisals for the Munich massacre he had reproached Fatah and Sa'ika for not undertaking enough missions against Israel. That month, the Soviet Union flew in a consignment of machine guns, mortars and small arms to supply the Fatah arsenal at Al Hama, about four miles from Damascus. The same day the Soviet Foreign Minister, Mr. Gromyko, told the United Nations General Assembly: 'It is impossible to condone the acts of terrorism committed by certain elements from the Palestinian movement which have led notably to the tragic events in Munich.'

But terrorism from Syria is inevitable, with 6,000 fedayeen in the southern part of the country at the end of 1972. To the Israelis, 'Syria has always been the most belligerent, the most destructive and the most bloodthirsty.'* Syria is being incited to step up the terrorist war, notably by Libya, its voluble partner in the tripartite federation that also embraces Egypt. Syria feels the sting of this pressure, politically and financially. Consistently rejecting any idea of a political settlement the Syrian politicians have deprived themselves of options. They can only nod assent when Sadat talks of a war he cannot wage or when Ghadafi preaches terrorism he can afford to finance. The result is that the fedayeen cannot easily be denied facilities for action. With Syrian regular units, they were in battle with the Israelis in December 1972; the Syrians lost six Mig-21 aircraft and fifteen tanks. Planting mines and firing 3,000 shells into kibbutzim, the Syrians apparently hoped to allow fedayeen to edge forward. The attempt was abortive as all such attempts must be in the face of Israeli determination 'not to tolerate any encroachment by the terrorists'.†

---

* *Jerusalem Post*, November 29, 1972.
† Israeli general commanding Northern Front to correspondents.

8 *Agony in Gaza*

The situation in the overcrowded Gaza Strip has always been more serious than anywhere else in the occupied lands. This was largely because the Egyptians made no attempt to develop the area while they held it; they preferred to maintain it as an irritant to Israel. Soon after the Six-Day War an American Middle East expert wrote, '... in the Gaza Strip the [342,000] Arabs lived a wretched existence under the control of Egypt, but the Egyptians used them only for their own purposes as pawns, while keeping their power to a minimum. They were not admitted into Egypt proper. They were forced to fester there so that their misery and hatred might make them a bone in the throat of the Israelis....'*

When the Israelis occupied the area after the Six-Day War they at once encountered much more hostility than on the West Bank. More than four years later a British journalist found that the Egyptian plan had been successful: 'Gaza is the only place where the Palestine resistance at a terrible cost and with suicidal tenacity is worthy of the name.'† The significant point is that the greater cost was borne by the Arabs of Gaza, not the Israelis.

The Gaza networks were better organised than those on the West Bank for here the public was more sympathetic, more

---

* Hal Draper, an editor of *New Politics*, in a lecture given at Berkeley College, California, shortly after the outbreak of the third Arab–Israeli War, 1967.

† John de St. Jarre, *Observer*, August 1, 1971.

volatile and more genuinely revolutionary because of hardship under the Egyptian régime. By spreading terror and intimidation the terrorist cells cowed most of the local population, 198,000 of whom lived in refugee camps. They executed people suspected of collaboration with the Israelis and, to protect their own security, they murdered other Arabs who had given them shelter. Often they killed on the flimsiest of evidence. A schoolgirl took revenge on a boy who rejected her advances —she was very un-Arab in taking such an initiative—by reporting him to a terror group as a 'collaborator'. The terrorists, who suspected that she herself was an informer, strangled both of them on orders from a local leader, Mahmoud Basili.

In Gaza the epithet of 'terrorist' is more apt than in any other area of Israeli–Arab conflict, as illustrated by typical atrocities. On July 22, 1970 seven terrorists kidnapped an Arab suspected of 'collaboration' from his house in Jebalya and then went to his sister's house to look for her husband. As he was out they took the woman. At Jebalya crossroads they shot their captives and threw a grenade at them. The man was killed but the seriously wounded woman was rescued and taken to hospital. Some hours later a terrorist got into the hospital and shot the woman dead in bed.

PFLP men kidnapped the daughter of Sulayman al-Huzeil of the Beersheba Bedouin and shot her because she and her father were 'co-operating with the enemy' despite a PFLP warning not to do so.* Mohammed Moussa Yassin, better known as Abu Nimer, second-in-command of PFLP in the Gaza Strip, said in a televised interview that many murders committed by his own men were carried out to 'settle personal accounts'. Death sentences for which he was responsible were usually handed down by PFLP command; the usual reason was for 'collaboration'.

'By God,' Nimer said, 'I never really knew whether the men were indeed collaborators.... I believe they were victims of

* Iraqi News Agency, June 13, 1971, quoted by BBC Monitoring Service.

false accusations of collaborators.... In the past we used to warn people once or twice but now we kill immediately without any proof.' He said that relations between the various terrorist groups were bad and that gangs often hated one another. Some murders have been savage beyond belief. One terrorist in Gaza admitted to having hacked to pieces a family of six in the Shatti refugee camp because he suspected them of co-operation with the Israelis.

Early in 1971 the Israelis picked up two fedayeen members who carried lists of Arab residents of Gaza who were to be executed for unstated 'crimes'. The Israelis warned the people listed and offered help and protection but none accepted the offer because they could think of nothing they might have done to anger the fedayeen. Some of those warned of their danger were subsequently murdered because they ignored the warning.

Terrorists have killed many more of their own people than Israelis. Most bombs thrown at Israeli cars miss the target and then explode among Arab civilians. On February 1, 1971 fedayeen set off a bomb in a Gaza post office and injured 61 Arabs.

Those Gaza Arabs trying to make a living by working in Israel are considered collaborators and have been targets for the terrorists. By mid-1972 the organisations had killed nearly 300 of their own people and wounded 1,385—including many women and children; in the same time they killed 50 Israelis and wounded 350. The Israelis seemed reluctant to react until the 'Arroyo incident' of January 21, 1971. Recent immigrants from Britain, the Aroyo family took a short cut through Gaza on their way home from a visit to the Negev desert. A schoolboy of 15 flagged down the car as if asking for a lift and then lobbed a grenade into the back seat. It killed two children, Mark, aged 7, and Abigail, 4, and smashed their mother's spine. The Arab boy had been paid £6 for the attack.

In the Israeli swoop which followed 150 terrorists were

caught, including the grenade-throwing gang which had paid for the Arroyo murders. Large stocks of weapons were found and many terrorists were driven underground. Families of wanted men were deported to Abu Sneima, a lonely port on the western Sinai coast to stop them from giving aid to the wanted men.

The Israelis then instituted a radical new initiative, partly dismantling the larger camps and resettling the displaced refugees elsewhere. For more rapid searches, patrol roads were driven through the camps. With these and other security measures camp murders dropped radically. For instance, in June and July 1971, before the patrol roads became operative, 21 Gaza Arabs were killed and 166 wounded by terrorists; in September and October 6 Arabs were killed and 19 wounded.

Security has been aided by the availability of employment in Israel, the improvement of public facilities and the encouragement by Israeli capital of new industries. Also Gazans were permitted to take jobs on the West Bank which suffers a manpower shortage because of the attractions of working in Israel. An effective anti-terrorist measure in November 1971 was the issue of forge-proof identity cards. These cards contain colour photographs taken by Polaroid (instant) cameras and sealed in a plastic case. If the case is tampered with and the photograph comes into contact with the air the colour fades and changes. Every identity card also carries the bearer's thumbprint.

By the end of 1971 only about sixty terrorist leaders were still at large and by mid-1972 the Israelis could claim that grenade and shooting incidents were rare. All the terrorist organisations had fragmented and gone underground and only a handful of names remained on the wanted list that had contained more than a hundred a year earlier. Only 150 prisoners were being held in 'administrative detention' compared with the peak figure of 450. The total number of prisoners, including those held for investigation, was 1,600 compared with 3,500 at the height of tension in the Strip.

In May 1972 the Israeli government announced that the Gaza Strip would be included within the bounds of Israel, so that it could never again be transformed into a base for attacks on Israel. This would suit the great majority of Gazans, for their prosperity is much more assured under Israeli administration than it ever was under the Egyptians. The presence of so many people in Gaza's refugee camps and Israel's own economic and physical limitations in providing for their resettlement—Gaza is hardly a priority area—means that the territory cannot approach the standards of life on the West Bank. But, increasingly, people can come out on the streets without fear, move freely in their search for work and live in an atmosphere where the gunman is not dominant; this provides its own momentum towards a better existence for all the Strip's inhabitants.

The fedayeen organisations were ultimately defeated in the Gaza Strip because of their own excesses which alienated large parts of the Arab population; because they were isolated from their parent groups in Lebanon and Syria and simply because the Israelis were too clever in dealing with them.

The Israelis allowed me to interview some prisoners held in Gaza gaol—and on my own terms, as I wanted to avoid any possibility of their not being free to speak their minds. Some of these Gazan Arabs had been picked up within days of joining a terrorist organisation and said they had been 'betrayed'. A schoolteacher told me that he had been 'shamed' into joining PFLP by his pupils. He said he felt that he had let them down but my impression was that he was glad to have been captured before he could commit any terrorist act. Aged 30, married and with two children, he simply wanted to live peacefully. All these prisoners were disenchanted with Fatah, PFLP and the Popular Liberation Army. 'They are not fighting the Israelis,' one told me, 'but the Arabs.' I did not get the impression that he and other prisoners I interviewed wanted the movements to fight the Israelis. These men hold no hope of rescue by fedayeen or Arab regular military action. They are resigned to sitting out their prison term in the expectation of a more secure life when they come out.

Still, the Gaza Strip, despite reflections of sub-tropical beauty at points along the road, is certainly the most depressed area of UNRWA operations. UNRWA provides basic rations for 199,600 persons in the Strip and CARE (Co-operative for American Relief Everywhere), in co-operation with the Israeli authorities, provides a social welfare programme for feeding about 20,000 'economic refugees' who are ineligible for UNRWA assistance. Without this outside assistance, which the refugees must still supplement as they can by barter, the produce of small gardens and work when it is available, thousands would go hungry.

The citrus harvest brings seasonal income to many in the large group of refugees who are usually unemployed. Since the Israelis commenced administration in 1967 three additional citrus packing plants have been built in the Strip, and all four plants have come into operation, each offering employment to approximately 600 men.

About 40,000 refugees work in Israel itself, mainly in agriculture and construction where there is a shortage of unskilled and semi-skilled labour. But this employment is controversial; the fedayeen groups regard it as a form of collaboration—arguing that it has enabled Israel to release men for military purposes and to build homes for new Jewish immigrants. In 1971 buses and men waiting for them in the grey dawn were several times the target of grenade attacks. There were no attacks in 1972 and workers continued to commute into Israel and back, leaving the Strip by bus in the morning and returning before sundown.

By the end of 1972 there was no unemployment in Gaza, for the first time since 1948, and despite sporadic acts of violence much of the earlier tension seemed to have evaporated. But some Arabs would like to see the tension sustained. In October 1972 the Mayor of Gaza, Rashad Ashawa, refused an Israeli order to grant municipal services—sewage, water and cleaning facilities—to Shatti camp and its 40,000 residents. Mr. Ashawa said that 'granting services to the Palestinians in the camp would make them fully-fledged citizens and make them forget they were refugees'. This, he said, would delay the 'solution' of the Palestine problem. Mr. Ashawa's solution is basically the fedayeen one, the rising of the refugees against Israel, not the sane and practical answer of co-existence. The Israeli authorities said they had no intention of changing the camp residents' refugee status if they preferred this, nor would they interfere with the functioning of UNRWA. Apart from Shatti, all camps in the Gaza Strip had, by the end of 1972, been linked with the services of neighbouring Israeli municipalities, thus raising their hygienic standards. Mr. Ashawa was dismissed and replaced by an Israeli government official so that Shatti could get the same services

9 *Propaganda and Indoctrination*

Fedayeen propaganda is not radically different from that of the Arab governments except perhaps in its exaggerations about the effectiveness of military operations. It is based on six fundamentals, one of which is the inculcation of hatred for the Jews, or rather for the 'bad' Jews, the Zionists. The 'good' Jews may remain in Palestine when it is liberated, according to some propaganda, but when the publicists or other leaders drop their guard they make it clear that a Jewish presence will not long survive the liberation process.

Another fundamental tenet is the use of slogans; neither Mao nor any American presidential candidate has used slogans so liberally as fedayeen publicists. The third main aspect of propaganda has been the attempt to rouse support for the 'Palestinian entity'—itself a slogan—by various indoctrination devices. The fourth is aimed at discrediting the Israelis, especially in allegations of torture of captured fedayeen. The fifth and most obvious propaganda gambit is the publication of misleading photographs and reports. And the sixth and most subtle is the plan to make the whole business of 'liberation' or 'resistance' into an institution, thus giving it status among educated, well-informed foreigners. Fatah and the other groups have learned that it is more important to influence those who influence public opinion than to attempt to influence public opinion directly.

Hatred was evident before Fatah became operational, as in

the writings of Nasir ad-Din an-Nashashibi, who is often quoted by some fedayeen leaders:

'I shall see the hatred in the eyes of my son and your sons. I shall see how they take revenge. If they do not know how to take revenge I shall teach them. And if they agree to a peace or a truce I shall fight against them as I fight against my enemy and theirs. I want them to be callous, to be ruthless, to take revenge. I want them to wash away the disaster of 1948 with the blood of those who prevent them from entering their land. Their homeland is dear to them, but revenge is dearer. We'll enter their lairs in Tel-Aviv. We'll smash Tel Aviv with axes, guns, hands, fingernails and teeth.... We shall sing the hymns of the triumphant, avenging return....'*

'The hatred which we indoctrinate into the minds of our children from their birth is sacred,' stated the Syrian Minister of Education, Suleyman Al-Khash, in a letter to M. René Maheu, Director-General of UNESCO.† In Palestinian schools, virtually all UNRWA financed, the whole philosophy of education is permeated with anti-Jewish material, much of it taken direct from textbooks sponsored by the Arab countries. Since large noses are common among Arabs the 'Jewish nose' is avoided in many caricatures; instead Jews are shown as ugly, puny, deformed and vicious people, resembling vultures, bats or mice. The atlas in common use ignores the existence of Israel, which is included in the 'Hashemite Kingdom and Palestine'. Yet, on the back of a standard exercise book appears a map of Israel. The Arab armies are shown encircling it and a missile is aimed at Tel Aviv.

A Syrian book contains this passage: 'The persecution of Jews in Europe is justified. The Jews were persecuted

* *Return Ticket*, Beirut, 1962.
† Reproduced in *A-Thaura*, Ba'ath Party journal, Damascus, May 3, 1968.

and despised because of their corruption, manners and treachery.... Jews are scattered to the end of the earth since by their nature they are wild, and enemies of mankind. What is the solution? I have heard it many times: "Atbach al Yahud [Slaughter the Jews]." '

The Jordan Ministry of Education produced a textbook, *Glances At Arab Society*, in which the following exercise is set. ' "Israel was born to die." Prove it!' This is in accord with a slogan regularly broadcast to Fatah members: 'From Q [H.Q.?] to the insurgents: "Exterminate, exterminate, exterminate!" '* 'Contribute a dinar and you have killed a Zionist,' encourages another Fatah slogan.

Palestine Liberation Radio broadcast this exhortation from Cairo on February 23, 1970: 'Our great masses! From the Voice of Palestine in Cairo we greet you and promise ... to continue the armed struggle and fulfil our blood-drenched duty—the duty to Jerusalem. We shall put an end to Zionist existence on the land of Palestine; we shall liberate all of Palestine by popular armed revolution.'

In some Fatah pronouncements are glimpses of a genocidal attitude, as in this explanation of why a conventional war does not suit the Palestinian goal:

'For the aim of this war is not to impose our will on the enemy but to destroy him in order to take his place [*ifna'uhu lil-hululi mahallahu*].... In a conventional war there is no need to continue the war if the enemy submits to our will ... while in a people's war there is no deterrent, for its aim is not to subjugate the enemy but to destroy [*ifna'*] him. A conventional war has limited aims which cannot be transcended, for it is necessary to allow the enemy to exist in order to impose our will over him, while in a people's war destruction of the enemy is the first and last duty.'

* Voice of Fatah, Cairo, February 18, 1970, quoted from BBC Monitoring Service.

The expression *ifna'* is extreme, its literal meaning being 'reduction to absolute nothingness'. This destruction does not refer to army units, as in military parlance, but to the enemy in order 'to take his place'.*

Fatah accepts that terrorism will increase the number of Jews wishing to leave Israel. In a public statement issued on the fifth anniversary of the beginning of Fatah activity (January 1, 1970) it was stated that guerrilla actions would spread to the heart of Israel's territory, and then the Israeli 'will find himself isolated and defenceless against the Arab soldier in his house, on his land, on the road, in the café, in the movie theatre, in army camps and everywhere, far from the area under control of the Israeli Air Force and mechanical equipment which assures him protection and security of life. These acts will force him to consider and compare the life of stability and repose that he enjoyed in his former country and the life of confusion and anxiety he finds in the land of Palestine. This is bound to motivate him towards reverse immigration.'†

Such unequivocal language draws criticism from abroad and hardly convinces even the non-Zionists that they should support the fedayeen cause, so by 1972 few fedayeen leaders were talking about 'annihilating Israel'. Arab language is rich and the propagandists have evolved many ways of presenting their case in an apparently moderate way. Euphemism is the principal device; propaganda speaks of 'liberating Palestine' or 'abolishing the entity of Israel', or says, 'In the Middle East there is no place for the Arab countries and Israel together.'

The reverse of the Israeli entity is the 'Palestinian entity', a slogan which became a tool in the hands of most Arab states. Its only significant outcome was the awakening of Palestinian nationalist feelings. At first dependent on Arab governments, 'Palestinian entity' took on an identity of its own; Nasser, in striving to create a Palestinian organisation that would

* *The Palestinian Revolution*, the Fatah monthly, June 1968, p. 38.
† *The Palestinian Revolution*, January 1970, p. 8.

depend on Egypt in every way, kindled feeings he could not control.

Slogans are easily comprehended, easily digested, easily remembered and repeated, hence their value to the propagandist. One of Fatah's favourite slogans is the Mao doctrine that 'Justice and peace comes from the cannon's mouth.' Other oft-quoted sayings include 'Long live an Arab Free Palestine' and 'A lay, democratic, pluralistic Palestine'—used to show the Israelis that the 'good' Jews will be given a place in the Middle East sun. Fatah used 'Struggle and Sacrifice' in a manifesto to the United Nations and it caught on among Palestinians. PFLP used a wordier slogan: 'Building up the fighting party, every fighter is a politician, every politician is a fighter.'

A Fatah writer produced a hymn of sacrifice:

> Farewell, tears and sorrow,
> Farewell, sighs and grief,
> Welcome, blood and heroic death,
> Welcome El-Asifa, who brings death and ruin
>   to our enemies;
> Welcome, the heroes of Salame and Tiberias
>   the Triangle and Beersheba,
> Now they return to the battlefield....

From slogans and hymns it is only a short step to aphorisms and extravagant language. 'Violence will purify the individuals from venom, redeem the colonised from their inferiority complex and restore courage to the native.'* Similarly: 'The Palestinian Revolution should continue to reiterate its conviction and belief that armed struggle is not an end in itself but a means to a great humanitarian end.'†

Fedayeen leaders believe the proverb-sounding utterance to be particularly effective. These are some examples:

* From a Fatah pamphlet, *Revolution and Violence: The Road to Victory.*
† *From Revolution Until Victory*, PLO booklet.

91

We are faced by a treacherous enemy, steeped in hatred and hostility, who knows only the language of force and violence.

The world never pities victims. It only honours victorious fighters.

Death in action for the annihilation of the enemy is preferable to the wait for a slow and miserable death for the sake of life.

Fatah's fighters specialise in the art of death for the sake of life.

To claim suffering at the hands of 'imperialism', is, like 'colonialism', a slogan well calculated to win sympathy among the many millions of other races who felt they too had suffered. A fedayeen leader told me: 'Of course Israel is neither imperialistic nor colonialistic—not by the widest stretching of definition—but by charging Israel with imperialism we can also say that Fatah is Vietnam, Fatah is Cuba, Fatah is Bolivia, Fatah is Algeria.'

Dr. Yehoshafat Harkabi (one-time Chief of Israeli Intelligence) maintains that the Palestinians call the conflict with Israel 'a war of national liberation' not for any objectively analysable reason but under the impact of psychologically understandable motives—because of 'an inclination to project it [the war of liberation] backwards and describe the conflict as if the Palestinians had waged continuous popular guerrilla warfare against the Jews'. In this way, Harkabi reasons, 'Heroism anticipated in the future is reinforced for inspiration drawn from the past.' The past itself is retouched to enable Palestinians to proclaim themselves 'not only imitators of Mao and Che but [to have] preceded them'. There is much truth in his analysis.

In its own documents the PLO notes: 'The strategic political slogans put forward by the national liberation movements and the national democratic revolutions in the age of imperialism are "revolutionary ideology", "strong organising party", "revolution led by workers and peasants", "a wide united national front" and "a war of popular liberation and long term resistance".'* The use of the term 'resistance' (*muqawama*) is interesting because it is really a falsehood by terminology, motivated by the psychological need to suggest that the Arab people actively resist the foreign intruder. Except in Gaza the Arabs have a negative attitude to the Israeli occupation but the occasional demonstration and verbal criticism is elevated by calling it 'resistance'.

Before the Six-Day War the principal slogans had been 'inch by inch', 'popular liberation war' and 'the policy of scorched earth'.† But by February 1969 the PFLP was questioning the value of these and other slogans. 'Is it justifiable to allow the reiteration of such statements as "We are all commandos", "All classes of the Palestinian people are waging the war of armed struggle" and "No rich and no poor as long as we are all landless"—without submitting these statements to close judgment, critical analysis, and preventing them from becoming widespread?'‡

The organisations have done their cause great harm with the repetition of slogans, as an Arab East Jerusalem editor observed: 'The guerrilla organisations have made their slogans without consulting anybody in the occupied territories, with the result that they have drowned themselves and the Palestinian people in oceans of fantasies and in a lack of realism, which has resulted in many tragedies.'§

The intellectuals' exploitation of the workers and peasants—which the PFLP at least sees as 'the classes of the revolution on the Palestinian battlefield'—is calculated and deliberate. The group's manifesto of February 1969 makes this clear. 'When one appeals to the workers and peasants—inhabitants

---

* *Basic Political Documents of the Armed Palestine Resistance Movement*, PLO Research Centre, Beirut, 1969, p. 223.
† Ibid, p. 128.
‡ Ibid, p. 200.
§ *Al-Quds*, August 8, 1971.

of camps, villages and city slums—and makes them politically aware, provides them with the organisation and means of fighting, then one will find the material and the solid base for an historical revolution of liberation. The setting up of this solid backbone to the revolution will make it possible for class alliance to be made which will serve the revolution's purpose without exposing it to vacillation, deviation or abortion.'*

One effective technique has been to find rapid explanations to fit crises as they occur. At one time trials in Israel revealed that Fatah terrorists captured on the West Bank had betrayed local residents who had sheltered them. Fatah's radio commentator at once announced that the whole thing was a plot: dark-skinned Israelis, pretending to be terrorists, had obtained food and shelter in Arab homes and then reported them to the Israeli police. Similarly, a spate of Fatah attacks on Arab residents in Gaza and Jericho was at once denounced as another Israeli trick to cause ordinary Arabs to distrust the fedayeen fighters.

Other methods of propaganda have been inept. Before the Six-Day War fedayeen leaders allowed recruits to tattoo their arms with the drawing of a mosque and the inscription, in Arabic, 'Allah, Palestine, coming back.' This made identification easy for the Israelis. Again, Fatah was long in discovering that it was a mistake to publish casualty lists in the Press and to sing the praises of newly dead fedayeen over the Voice of Fatah from Cairo Radio. Both practices tended to discourage volunteers.

An intriguing aspect of propaganda has been the effort by all the fedayeen groups and their supporting organisations, such as the PLO Research Centre, to sell the idea that Israel suffers greater military casualties than it will admit; also, that these casualties are hidden as 'road accidents'.

* *Basic Political Documents of the Armed Palestine Resistance Movement*, PLO Research Centre, Beirut, 1969, pp. 194-5.

Israel systematically announces the names of Service fatalities. Even one omission is impossible as the whole neighbourhood from which the dead man came would know of his death—through his family—and public confidence would be destroyed. The Israelis feel their casualties, for Israel considers itself one big family and mourns every loss. Families advertise their bereavements in the newspapers and in Israeli society it would be virtually impossible to hide casualties. The policy of complete revelation of casualties has in any case been generally advantageous to the Israeli administration—the Israeli public likes to be in the know—but it was disadvantageous during the 'war of attrition' because as some government advisers believed, it probably was harmful to morale for the public to be glued to hourly news broadcasts to learn what new casualties had occurred. But the practice continued.

Some intensive propaganda has been aimed at the Arabs resident in Israel—the so-called Israeli Arabs—440,000 of them in 1972. About 130,000 live in 65 towns and villages of Galilee and 50,000 in 27 villages of the Triangle—the area east of Tel Aviv. Others live in the cities of Haifa and Acre. The fedayeen leaders tried sporadically to set up cells among Israeli Arabs, but with little success beyond some sabotage acts in the cities. When propaganda failed to win recruits for cells within Israel the movement resorted to recruiting by terror. A wealthy Arab from Acre was forced to co-operate with a Fatah cell set up in his area after fedayeen killed one of his children in front of him and threatened to kill his wife and their other children.

From a humanitarian point of view, the worst aspect of fedayeen propaganda and indoctrination remains the steeping of Palestinian children in 'sacrifice', violence and revenge. 'The Palestine Pupil's Motto' is prominently displayed—in English —in most UNRWA schools.

Palestine is our home
To return home is our target
To struggle is our way
Education is our light
Faith is our sword
Sacrifice is our duty
Union is our explorer
Work is our constitution
Discipline is our motto
Martyrs are our leaders
Death doesn't frighten us
Palestine ours ours ours

In the grounds of the Ein el-Hilweh Elementary School, in south Lebanon, are the graves of four young fedayeen killed during fighting with the Lebanese Army. Surrounded by iron railings, the graves have the appearance of a monument and bear the inscription: 'They spilled their blood; don't be afraid to look on it; don't spare your blood.' Ritualistic ceremonies are frequently held here and on the rafters of the same school is the sign 'God will save the Palestinians.' Education of the present Arab generation in vengeance and brutality, though directed outward, could rebound and take heavy toll within the Arab states.

The fedayeen organisations are possibly in the process of becoming a sect. This is certainly so of the Ashbal—the 'Lion Cubs' or junior fedayeen. Boys between the ages of 6 and 15 are systematically recruited into Ashbal, which is potentially the most revolutionary element in the fedayeen movement. 'We are not just a paramilitary organisation,' an Ashbal leader told me in Lebanon. 'This is a morale-building and educational movement to prepare the well-rounded citizen of Palestine—equipped and trained to defend his nation but also to be a good, productive citizen.' During training the boys chant, 'Oh Zionists, do you think you are safe? Drinking blood is a habit of our men.' They undergo a Mau Mau-like hardening course in which each boy is required to tear apart a live chicken to develop a lust for killing.*

After their daily lessons in refugee camp schools the Ashbal run to parade and for several minutes their instructors drill them. The movements are simple but like everything else about Ashbal, highly political. When ordered to stand at ease, they shout '*Asifa!*' (Storm). When they stamp to attention they bellow '*Fatah!*'

The instructors are either former school-teachers or wounded guerrillas, men who are almost deified. Part of the training ritual is the frequent morale-building talk by a feda'i supposedly just back from a mission. The boys are taught to dismantle, clean and re-assemble rifles, pistols and machine guns and are allowed to fire live ammunition aimlessly, so that it becomes a pleasure. Then they are given targets, and are taught to fire Decteriov light machine guns at aircraft. At the end of training sessions the boys stand stiffly to attention and chant their Fatah credo: 'I have shattered the manacles —limiting my freedom and I have arisen like a hurricane to break out of my prison and free my country.' They have no standard uniform but some wear the black and white chequered head-cloth adopted by Fatah fighters or a camouflage Castro cap.

Their first task when building a camp is to dig a slit trench for mock battles in which they play at storming an Israeli outpost. By 1969 a major component of popular culture was a highly stylised and coloured account, published almost daily in the newspapers, of how this or that commando section over-ran an Israeli position, 'killing all the Zionists inside with blades', or 'repulsing gigantic reinforcements including helicopter gunships'. The Ashbal's favourite pastime and sport is acting out this legend. Each 'raid' reaches its climax as the attacking group storms the enemy position, shouting, 'We are

* John M. Mecklin, *Fortune*, June 1970.

from Fatah! We have come to kill you all!' An adult instructor fires live rounds to increase the excitement.

In their camps, the boys nail up cardboard from ration boxes and scrawl slogans such as 'Our revolution is a drop of blood, a drop of sweat and a drop of ink.' Older boys go on ten-mile marches at weekends, shouting 'To Palestine! To Palestine!'

The motive for it all was explained by a school-teacher instructor: 'We teach them that the Palestinian people are a great people and that they have the strength, in the end, after many battles, to win back the land. The little ones must understand.... We teach them that behind Israel is American imperialism. We teach them that we are not struggling for the love of struggling but for the love of the land.'

But because of their policy of non-recognition of Israel, the Palestinians know very little of the land they love. Even educated, top-level fedayeen leaders reveal an abysmal ignorance. They know nothing of Israel's economy, population structure, labour organisations, educational system, social life or its government. They do not want to learn, perhaps because they are frightened of finding out that Israel is too stabilised to be moved. Perhaps, too, the leaders' ignorance indicates that their primary interest is in using Israel to foment an inter-Arab revolution. Yet after the war of 1967 many Arabs attributed their defeat to lack of knowledge of Israel. Even now what little knowledge they possess is distorted to fit preconceived ideas. Thus, fedayeen leaders have told me that Israel's nationalism is artificial and hybrid that the Jews 'are a religion and not a race'. Because of this, they say, the Jews' attachment to their state is weak and that the state will crumble under the first reverse.

Fatah is on stronger ground in its more humanitarian activities. For instance, it established the Palestinian Red Crescent, a form of Red Cross organisation—though the Red Cross itself could not recognise the organisation because of its belligerent connections. For a long time Fatah aided the families of fallen saboteurs, educated their children, smuggled funds to families of Fatah members in prison on the West Bank or in Gaza. This aid was supposed to be for life but many of the benefits had dried up by 1972.

A favourite propaganda ploy has been to liken the Israeli Jews to the Nazis. This profoundly angers the Israelis, but it is only fair to point out that no Arab feels the sort of guilt or shame that every Westerner feels, or is impelled to show that he is feeling, for the horrible chapter in human history—the maltreatment of the Jews in Europe. For a Palestinian Arab, therefore, it is not taboo to attempt to make comparisons between the German and Israeli occupations. However, in making such comparisons the fedayeen propagandists show great naïveté and little professionalism, for throughout the Western world the Arab practice has in general only produced greater support for the Israelis. This is not to deny the considerable sympathy for the Palestinian refugees, but the fedayeen excesses have gradually eroded this.

Clovis Maksoud, deputy editor of *Al-Ahram*, chided the fedayeen leaders: 'The Palestinian revolution needs to be exposed to ideas and people; what it needs is not public relations but relations with the public.'*

The fedayeen are generally presented by their own propaganda as men living near the poverty line. This is true of the rank and file though they get a regular salary. It is also true that many of the fedayeen leaders, notably Habash, are not financially corrupt. But the resources of the movement at large are immense. In 1970 the business magazine *Fortune* authoritatively estimated that Fatah's war chest stood at 25 million US dollars and that its annual income was 10 million US dollars.

The financial structure is complicated and to some extent each organisation has its own finances. Saudi Arabia gives money to Fatah but not to the PLO because this would imply

* In a speech to the Palestinian Symposium, Kuwait, February 1971.

recognition of the associated fedayeen groups which Saudi Arabia dislikes. Much money comes in to PLO from the Palestine National Fund, the tax imposed on all Palestinians living outside the 'war area'. This is then distributed.

Arafat has worked constantly to get all Arab countries to bring in direct taxation for the benefit of Fatah. He has not been successful but several countries, notably Kuwait, make budgetry provision for the terrorists. Most Arab countries levy a two per cent 'fedayeen tax' on all entertainment tickets.

The most reactionary Arab rulers subsidise the proponents of social revolution as a shrewd investment, for otherwise dangerous revolutionary fervour is thus channelled into an exclusively anti-Israel direction. This diverts the revolutionaries from truly revolutionising Arab society. Ready parallels would be having the Vietcong financed by the Saigon millionaires or a Castro getting his monthly cheque from Standard Oil. Other money is extorted from wealthy Palestinian businessmen, but to what extent this is sanctioned by fedayeen hierarchy is not clear. It is possible that extremists and local terrorist leaders practise extortion and blackmail without orders from their headquarters.

Early in 1972 Fatah paid its members 150 to 500 Lebanese pounds (15 to 50 pounds sterling) a month according to the number of dependents, but called the allotment an 'appropriation' rather than a wage because Fatah work is not considered employment but a kind of spiritual activity. In an Arab country this is a high salary. The Popular Front and Popular Democratic Front pay was 75 to 150 Lebanese pounds, depending on family commitments; officers are paid the same as men. A Beirut office boy gets about this amount. Sa'ika fedayeen are better paid than all others, while men of the Palestine Liberation Army are paid the same as the soldiers of most Arab armies.*

* These figures were given to the author by Ibrahim Al-Abid of the PLO Research Centre, Beirut.

10 *Loss of Credibility*

Among their own people the fedayeen organisations have lost more credibility as a result of false or exaggerated claims of victories than through defeats at the hands of the Israelis and the Jordanians. Fatah's operational career began with a false claim and the history of the entire fedayeen movement is littered with clumsy lies and extravagances.

In the four years from June 1967 to June 1971 the fedayeen organisations officially claimed to have killed 8,619 Israeli soldiers and civilians, destroyed 351 tanks, 88 aircraft, 5,331 vehicles and 312 bridges. Such catastrophic losses, had they occurred, would have badly damaged Israel's morale and fighting potential. Caustically commenting on these figures the Beirut newspaper, *Al-Jarida*, noted that Israel did not possess 312 bridges.

On May 10, 1968 Fatah claimed (Communiqué 116) that a saboteur group killed all the guards at Al Dabassiye camp, destroyed four army dormitories and killed all soldiers sleeping in them. They then retired, routing in the process an Israeli reinforcement group. Such an operation would have called for a large conventional raiding force. Exploiting the 'victory', a Fatah spokesman announced in the Kuwaiti *Al-Risala* (March 11, 1968) that if the Arab states gave a free hand to Fatah and the other organisations they would crush Israel in three years.

Sometimes, as many as five terrorist groups would claim

credit for one raid, disregarding Arab world anger and ridicule elsewhere. Habash and his PFLP colleagues were the principal offenders and Damascus radio labelled them 'a parasitic group that lives by robbing others of their due honour'. Few Arabs will criticise the fedayeen to other Arabs, but one who did so was Ibrahim Bakr, a former Deputy Chairman of PLO. In March 1969 Bakr said: 'The Arab information services exaggerate the terrorists' deeds.... This might cause considerable damage to the fedayeen activity since it places greater responsibility than it could possibly carry.... The publicity campaign comforts the masses but when frustration sets in, when we stand in danger of being destroyed, they will not embrace us with enthusiasm.' Bakr was soon removed from office.

One of the most remarkable false claims was made by Arafat himself, then Abu Ammar. The Israeli Defence Forces had held a parade through Jerusalem on May 2, 1968, an event important enough to draw hundreds of newspapermen and foreign television crews. The entire uneventful parade was shown live on Israeli TV. Arafat announced:

'Overcoming the strong security precautions of the enemy, which included 30,000 soldiers supported by 60 helicopters and fighter squadrons, a suicide force from Group 387 managed to reach the rear of the military parade and to shell it with mortars and rockets. This resulted in heavy losses to the enemy's forces. The maddened enemy now moved immense numbers of troops in order to encircle our heroic forces. Battle was waged north-west of Jerusalem and our fighters used hand grenades, machine guns and anti-tank weapons. Our forces destroyed a number of tanks which were seen to go up in flames. Israel's losses in soldiers were not less than 30 killed and wounded. Four of our heroic fighters were killed while the rest retired safely to base....'

News of the exploit reached the United Nations where the

Secretary General, U Thant, stated: 'As far as I know there occurred no incidents during the military parade in Jerusalem.'

Fatah announced that on May 25, 1969 in a dawn attack on an enemy camp north-east of Jericho 120 Israeli officers and soldiers were killed or wounded and much damage done to transport and equipment, while fedayeen losses were two injured. This remarkable victory was based on a clash between an Israeli platoon and a group of 12 fedayeen; three were killed and one was captured while two wounded were dragged to safety under supporting fire from Jordanian artillery. The Israelis had one man killed and two wounded.

Abu Ayad admitted in June 1969 that fedayeen claims were grossly exaggerated. 'In the Jordan Valley every week five or six tanks are blown up by the principal organisations. [Ayad might more accurately have said 'attacked' rather than 'blown up'.] Yet every small organisation claims these operations for itself. If the minimum number of these organisations is six or seven, the total number of tanks blown up according to communiqués will be at least 24. This is the basis of regrettable exaggeration.'

At one time Fatah ordered each fighter in an action to submit a detailed report on the operation and enemy losses; the debriefing officer then calculated an average. This, too, was usually unrealistically high. Fedayeen have admitted to me that they discussed the operation on the return journey and came to an agreed figure for casualties. 'We would have been in trouble if we did not claim to have killed a reasonable number of Israelis,' one man told me.

In their weekly newspaper, *Fateh*, October 24, 1969, Fatah claimed that its commandos had launched 68 operations in one week, the actions ranging from the planting of time bombs in a Tel-Aviv leather factory to destruction or damage to 37 military vehicles; 14 ambushes, attacks on barracks and posts, seven bridges and railway lines, one ammunition depot, seven different installations, a water pump and an electricity line, an observatory, radar station and three observation posts. In addition rockets and bombs were fired at settlements. In an exhaustive study of foreign and Israeli newspapers, radio transcripts and official reports I could find no more than six Fatah operations for the same week.

The Syrian organisation, Sa'ika, claimed that on December 17, 1969 a patrol ambushed an Israeli force and killed, among others, Colonel Gideon Bandal, senior instructor in the Israeli military college, Captain Yitshaq, chief of staff of the northern region, 36 Israeli military cadets and 5 soldiers.[*] Fatah also claimed to have killed Bandal, though at a different place. The truth is that the colonel was killed in a road accident at a crossroads on the Ta'anakh–Yizrael road. The ambush of the cadets was a fabrication.

The Israelis have diverted themselves on at least four occasions by broadcasting over their Arabic-language Voice of Israel an announcement about some fictitious sabotage operation. All the major fedayeen groups have fallen into the trap, instantly claiming the 'operation' and usually embellishing it.

PFLP made the most extravagant claim of all, announcing on December 17, 1969 that its men had attacked on a front the length of 12 Israeli settlements. This would have been a major military operation and even the Palestinian Armed Struggle Command announced that it was sceptical of the claim. As reprisal for the 'insult' the PFLP froze its membership in the ASC.

One of Fatah's boldest claims concerned the 'battle of Auja' in 1970 where 48 commandos were said to have defeated 2 battalions of Israelis (about 1,000 soldiers) inflicting 65 casualties for a loss of 7 fedayeen. In another battle at Auja 26 fedayeen took on an Israeli battalion, killing 45 enemy for a further loss of 7 fedayeen.[†] Another famous Fatah

---

[*] Damascus Radio, in Arabic, 0515 GMT January 12, 1970; from the BBC Monitoring Service.

[†] From the Fatah handbook, *Political and Armed Struggle*, Beirut, 1970.

announcement was its claim to have wounded Defence Minister Moshe Dayan; he had actually been injured during archaeological excavations—and in full view of many people. Similarly, Fatah claimed to have killed Prime Minister Levi Eshkol after he had died in bed following a long illness.

In a sense, the organisations have been forced to claim victories. Their financial sponsors, principally Saudi Arabia and Kuwait and later Libya, wanted to see some result from the vast sums of money expended. For several years, too, it was possible to stimulate faltering fund-raising drives by claiming notable victories. Also, recruits were more easily brought into the movements by exciting reports of fedayeen supremacy in battle.

An Egyptian editor has noted that, 'When we Arabs praise some imaginary deed, we are carried away by the same feeling of satisfaction that we would feel if we had really carried it out.'* And a Lebanese editor was reprimanding the fedayeen when he wrote: 'We have tried to lie many times—and it has brought about only destruction. Perhaps we should try, just once, to tell the truth.'†

Captured individual fedayeen carry their exaggerations into their trials before Israeli courts. Baghdad-born Farouk Karim el-Shamiri was charged in 1972 on nine counts of terrorism, including murder. He protested that he had killed 28 Israeli soldiers—many more than charged—in revenge for the death of his father, an Iraqi officer, killed during an Israeli raid in northern Jordan in 1967. He also claimed that fedayeen were under orders to shoot their own wounded in the field because this gave the group greater mobility.

Of all the claims the one which deserves the most serious analysis is that which likens the Palestinian fedayeen war to the Algerian war of independence and to other 'wars of liberation'. Other Arabs have made the same assumption as

* *Al-Ahram*, October 26, 1969.
† *El-Jihad*, February 6, 1970.

105

did General Sweidani, Syrian Chief of Staff, in 1967:

'The situation in Palestine *differs* [Sweidani's emphasis] from that in Vietnam or Algeria only if we view Palestine as the homeland of a non-Arab people. But if we see Palestine as it is—a part of Arab territory taken over by imperialism, as if this land had occupied a part of Vietnam—we shall then realise that the situation in Palestine is quite similar to that in Vietnam or Algeria.... We believe that the Palestine arena, symbolising the great Arab catastrophe that has moved and tensed the nerves of a whole people can give birth to the longed-for unity.... He who liberates Palestine will lead the Arab nation towards an all-embracing unity. He who kindles the popular war of liberation will have power to cast all reactionary régimes *in the Arab world* [my italics] into the sea.'

In its statement to the United Nations General Assembly on October 15, 1968, Fatah stressed that the Palestine Resistance Movement was very similar to the heroic resistance movements in the German occupation of several European countries during World War II—France, Italy, Poland, Czechoslovakia, the Soviet Union, Yugoslavia, Rumania and others. 'The allied nations, and the Free World, considering these resistance movements to be just, lawful, sacred and deserving support by all free men, hastened to support them by all ways and means. Fatah, therefore, is at a loss to understand why certain European and American countries take a stand towards the Palestine resistance movement, utterly and diametrically opposed to the stand taken towards the European resistance movements.'

The disparity between the Algerian and Palestinian cases has been best expressed by Arabs themselves, notably Naji Alush and Professor Walid Khalidi. 'The legend of the liberation of Algeria may push the liberation of Palestine into an abyss,' Alush wrote. 'The heroic triumph of the Algerian revolt made some Palestinians and some progressive Arabs fancy that following the same road will bring the same results.'

These are the differences, from an analysis by Professor Khalidi expanded by Alush before the Six-Day War.

1. *The Combat Area.* Algeria was a colony with a small French minority and 10,000,000 Algerians. Palestine is divided into three: a small Arab minority in Israel concentrated in a few zones, and limited in its possibilities of action; the West Bank has become a Jordanian colony occupied by the 'Forces of the Desert and mercenaries', where the Palestinians are prohibited from organizing themselves; the Gaza Strip is administered as occupied territory by an Arab government, withholding from its inhabitants self-government which might have transformed them into a nucleus from which serious action for the liberation of Palestine could have been developed. The Palestinians in Gaza and the West Bank have first to overcome Arab government domination, before they can organize themselves for war.

2. *The Nature of the Battle.* In Algeria it was a battle for independence ... which is not the case in Palestine. There it is a battle for the uprooting of a state recognized by the United Nations, supported by world public opinion and the principal capitalist states.... Britain and the United States were ready to accept the independence of Algeria, but they are not ready to accept the liquidation of the Zionists' state. The Algerian struggle for independence could be compared to the Palestinians' struggle before 1948 ... after 1948 the nature of the situation changed in Palestine.

3. Algerians could have bases in Tunisia and Morocco. However, no Arab government will tolerate the organization of the Palestinians on its territory, unless they constitute a part of its forces and are subservient to its policy.

4. *The Problem of Power.* The Algerian people could paralyse, by employing guerrilla warfare, a large French army, owing to the vastness of Algeria which is 852,600 square miles, in which there were many mountains, thick scrub and forest, and roadless regions, which rendered movement of the army difficult and made way for successful guerrilla warfare. As regards little Palestine, most of the occupied territory is a plain, settled with fortified settlements, connected by an extensive network of roads, which facilitates army movements and renders the task of fedayeen difficult.

5. When the revolution erupted in Algeria, its active organizations were in Algeria. As regards the Palestinians, the organization of a revolution must grow outside the occupied territory.... Since the revolutionary organizations are outside the boundaries of the Zionists' state, any action by them necessitates an armed invasion.... The usurping state will then launch a military operation against the Arab neighbouring countries.

6. In Algeria, the fighters were men attached to their people who left the towns and their sham for the bosom of the masses. The propagandists of revolution in Palestine are chatterboxes of the bourgeoisie who prefer coffee houses in Beirut, Damascus, or Gaza to the sands of the occupied territory and the mountains of what was left in Palestine west of the Jordan. They organize themselves in Gaza, Lebanon, and Kuwait issuing thousands of proclamations without remembering once where the battlefield is, or discovering its boundaries and purpose.

7. Arab states' aid to Algeria was very small, yet, despite its smallness, Algeria achieved victory because her conditions made that meagre aid sufficient. However, in the battle for Palestine, the aid will not be adequate even if it is large. This is because the aim is to uproot the usurping state and not to spread fear and ruin inside its borders. The Palestinian people, divided and oppressed, cannot mobilize the necessary power

to squash the Zionists' state which is defended by 300,000 well-trained and well-armed soldiers.

8. The Algerian campaign took a territorial shape (i.e. pertaining to one Arab people or state ... the struggle stopped at the traditional borders of Algeria, and it recognized the borders drawn by colonialism. This nature of territoriality made the Palestinians demand a territorial struggle (i.e. by the 'Palestinian entity' as distinct from the rest of the Arabs), but that is impossible in Palestine. Algeria could be liberated without a clash with Tunisia or Morocco and their reactionary governments, while the revolutionary operation for the liberation of Palestine must collide with the Government of Jordan.

A year after the Six-Day War, on August 18, 1968, the editor of the Egyptian *Al-Ahram*, Mohammed Heikal, Egypt's leading editor, pointed to striking differences between the Palestinian campaign and those in Algeria and Vietnam:

1. The human ratio between the resistance forces and the enemy in the occupied territory is not like the ... ratio ... in Algeria ... ten million Arabs against an enemy of four hundred thousand French soldiers. In Palestine inside the occupied area the Arabs are less than a million and the enemy are two million with a quarter of a million under arms. [All Heikal's figures are inaccurate but they show the disadvantage of the Arabs in the 'occupied' areas compared with the advantages of the Algerians.]

2. The nature of the Palestinian terrain is different from ... Algerian terrain with its rugged mountains.... In Palestine the plains are exposed and the mountains are not spacious. Furthermore, the Palestinian land is limited and narrow, in particular taking into account the extensive use of helicopters.

3. Around Vietnam there are sanctuaries in which resistance can prepare itself out of the enemy's reach, such as China and North Vietnam. The situation was similar in Algeria,

with Tunisia and Morocco next door, and Libya and Egypt close by. The Palestinian resistance does not have such sanctuaries in which it can prepare itself out of reach of the enemy. The enemy is prepared to strike at any place in the Arab world, which in the present situation is defeated and has not yet recovered its strength.

There are yet other differences not mentioned by Arab writers:

1. The fedayeen leaders have virtually no plans or even ideas for Palestine after its liberation—in contrast to the FLN (National Liberation Front) leaders who debated the future image of liberated Algeria throughout its years of struggle.
2. Every sentence passed on an Algerian nationalist, every reprisal caused scores of new nationalists to take up arms and resist—and each group tougher than those before. This has not happened with the Palestinians.
3. While the FLN could induce the French to relinquish their rule in Algeria, no amount of terrorism could force the French to give up France. Yet that is what the fedayeen hope to do to Israel.

There is, however, one striking similarity between the Algerian and Palestinian situations. The Algerians killed many more Algerians than Frenchmen; the Palestinians have killed more Palestinians than Israelis.

Algerians themselves see the differences which escape the Palestinians. Mohamed Yazid, an FLN leader and later Algerian ambassador to the Lebanon, noted some essential factors. 'In Algeria we started our armed struggle with the one fundamental position of unity of the resistance movement and we gave that a real priority, and we gave it as much thought as we did to the everyday fighting against the French.... [Also] we found it very important to use the surrounding countries as bases and from the first we co-operated with those countries

110

on a clear basis, i.e. non-intervention of the host country in our internal affairs and non-intervention in their internal affairs.'*

The object of guerrilla warfare, as the Algerians saw it, was to create a state of insecurity for the occupying forces. Militarily, they did not win their war against the French, but by creating acute and chronic insecurity they forced General de Gaulle to make a political decision on Algeria's independence

One of the Palestine fedayeen's great mistakes has been the assumption of success by precedent: that is, that the success of revolution or guerrilla warfare in China, Cuba, Algeria and Vietnam guarantees success for the fedayeen. They have hypnotised themselves with the main guerrilla treatises of Mao Tse-Tung, Giap, Che Guevara and Régis Debray, and Fatah spokesmen have many times explained that they have learned from their 'brothers' but rely on their own specific experience. This is apparently why they ignore Mao's advice that guerrilla warfare can succeed only in a large country where irregular fighters can establish a base out of reach of enemy forces. The fedayeen counter Mao by saying that Cuba is a success story of guerrilla warfare in a small country; they forget or ignore that Cuba has jungle vastnesses where large guerrilla forces can hide for years. Many other things make Cuba different, including a friendly population in which to hide. Guevara is not a happy example for the fedayeen leaders to choose. He could not see the differences between one country and another and lost his life because of them.

Similarly, the fedayeen ignore the counter-revolutionary success of the British in Malaya, the Portuguese in Angola and Mozambique, the French in Madagascar, the Indonesian élite and the bourgeoisie against the proletariat. They ignore the ability of the white South Africans to abort any revolution among the black South Africans. Indeed, fedayeen leaders do not read material which might tend to damage their preconceptions about guerrilla warfare.

* *Journal of Palestine Studies*, Winter 1972.

Fedayeen

Late in 1969 Hisham Sharabi wrote an entire thesis on the credibility and effectiveness of the Palestine guerrillas.* Conceding that before the Six-Day War the balance of credibility was overwhelmingly in favour of the Israelis, Sharabi believed that by the end of 1969 the balance had swung to the fedayeen. By January 1972 Sharabi admitted that the organisations had failed to hold their credibility and, as evidence, cited the changed attitude of Palestinians to the Voice of Fatah broadcasts from Cairo. In 1968-69 this was a favourite programme; by 1971 many Palestinians did not know that the broadcast was still going out.† It is a reasonable assumption that the Palestinians' disenchantment was the result of the hundreds of false extravagant claims. The fedayeen failure followed Sharabi's comment, written early in 1970: 'The movement is probably on the threshold of total popular involvement.'

But at the end of 1972 a veteran Yugoslav observer had a clearer perspective:

Years after its inception the movement has no clear and detailed social and political programme ... revealing itself as a patchwork of compromises and contradictions.... It differs essentially from similar undertakings by departing from the canon of a strong political foundation and by using the discontent of the masses exclusively to demonstrate an immediate military capacity.... There is the risk of such dangerous adventurism as terrorism becoming a substitute for purposeful activity.... The Palestinian movement is prey to nationally determined shifts of strategy on the part of Arab governments.‡

* *Palestine Guerrillas: Their Credibility and Effectiveness*, Center for Strategic and International Studies, Georgetown University, 1970. Reprinted by the Institute of Palestine Studies, Beirut, 1971.

† In a conversation with me, Beirut, January 1972.

‡ Mirko Aksentijevic, long-time Beirut correspondent for Tanjug News Agency, in *Journal of Palestine Studies*, Beirut, Autumn 1972.

11 *The Image and the Reality*

An extraordinary feature of the Israeli–Arab conflict in general and of the Israeli–fedayeen part of it in particular is that both sides claim that the Western Press favours the *other* side. Whatever the truth about the general situation, the specific one is clear enough. The fedayeen have had extraordinarily good publicity in the West—better than that given to Israel—being presented pretty much on their own terms as heroes and resistance fighters on the classic anti-Nazi pattern, a gallant few facing fearful odds. They were romanticised by the media in the United States, Britain and much of Europe to appear as idealistic daredevils and diehards.

Such an attitude by Press, Radio and Television was understandable, for by their very nature the information media deal in the spectacular and the colourful—and the fedayeen were both. Emerging from the desert in their Arab head-dress, giving every impression of being idealistically motivated—which many of them were—the fedayeen made good copy. This was especially so while the foreign commentators saw them as genuine freedom fighters ready to sacrifice all for love of homeland and apparently winning great victories against the powerful Israelis who had already vanquished the regular Arab armies. Indeed, the Western media gave every appearance, during Fatah's rise to power, of glorifying violence and romanticising the guerrilla.

Paradoxically, some Arab newspapers condemned violence, notably *Al-Quds*, the East Jerusalem Arab-language newspaper edited by a dedicated Arab nationalist, Mahmoud Abu Zuluf.

113

On November 24, 1968 terrorists put a bomb in a car and parked it in Machne Yehuda Market, Jerusalem, killing 12 people and injuring 51, both Jews and Arabs. Abu Zuluf's editorial read: 'There is no doubt that every man sound in his mind, Arab or Jew, will denounce this action and will regret the loss of innocent blood.... Here we might ask: Is it with such means that we can reach a peaceful solution which we all want so much? These terrible activities must be denounced by us, as they are repudiated by everybody who has the interests of this country at heart.'

The Israelis themselves contributed to fedayeen image-building, especially of Arafat. Contemptuous though they professed to be, the Israelis became obsessed by Arafat, repeating his declarations, listening to him on radio, watching him on television, discussing him in their clubs. They were exasperated by some Western reporting because it seemed to them that from the tone of their writing the reporters assumed that the fedayeen had a perfect moral right to slaughter Jews. A Fatah leader spoke to a British journalist who watched a group being briefed before a mission. 'They are going up country tomorrow,' he said. 'They have simple orders: Kill Jews! We don't care whether the dead are civilians or soldiers, just so long as they are Jews.' Telling the journalist the result of a raid, he said, 'Only two Jews killed tonight. Disappointing. Never mind, another two Jewish families will be in mourning.'*

During 1968 and 1969 the Western Press readily accepted fedayeen stories of famous victories. In Jordan a *Daily Telegraph* reporter met a feda'i who supposedly doubled as a Fatah Press Officer and a night-raider and in good faith reported what this feda'i told him.

> It had been a text-book exercise with no casualties; this was unusual as the guerrillas are resigned to a high casualty rate, operating as they have to, in nearly open country which is

* Bernard Jordan, *Daily Mail*, January 14, 1969.

sparsely populated. A party of 20 had crossed the River Jordan and attacked a newly-established Israeli outpost quite close to the river. While the main body had encircled the outpost two other groups had been stationed to the north and south on the main road. The attack with bazookas and mortars had opened up but had met unexpectedly strong opposition when the Israelis replied with a heavy machine gun.

Meanwhile, tank reinforcements had been summoned and were approaching from the north and south. But on this occasion the guerrillas were using efficient radio communication and the mortar scored a direct hit on the machine gun. Both the tank detachments were then successfully ambushed and the entire detachment was able to return across the river before reinforcements could be summoned. The Press Officer put his Beretta on the table and loosened his belt. It had been a peculiarly Near Eastern occasion with the guerrillas shouting Arabic battle cries and the trapped Israelis replying with loud obscenities. As far as he could judge all the soldiers in the outpost had died.*

By any military standards, this was quite an exploit—and one likely to be remembered in fedayeen legend. I have given many fedayeen opportunities to tell me about 'memorable attacks' but none produced this story. There is no mention of it in any Fatah communiqué, yet Fatah never missed reporting the slightest 'operation', such as the cutting of a telephone wire. It seems very probable that the story was created for the benefit of the reporter; it was certainly fortunate that a fedayeen Press Officer happened to be on the spot. For this *Daily Telegraph* reporter, visiting a Fatah training camp in Jordan, Fatah also produced a seven-year-old girl who recited a poem about returning to Palestine. The fedayeen showered her with apples and kisses and rewarded her with a forage cap. 'This is the generation that will reach the sea,' the journalist was told.

* Patrick Marnham, *Daily Telegraph* magazine, February 28, 1969.

Fedayeen

He wrote of the fedayeen: 'Guerrillas outrage every military sensibility. They don't shave, they don't stand up and fight. Instead they strike and run. They appear unexpectedly and make fools of stronger forces, and they kill indiscriminately and for political reasons.... They are volunteers and aggressors because without being fully committed and without attacking they will achieve nothing. So serious an enemy has to be seriously opposed.... Logically, one can expect the conflict ... to be fought more bitterly and ruthlessly every year....'*

Later that year another British reporter writing from Israel believed that the guerrillas had become 'a real and aggressive component in the Israeli nightmare'.† An American journalist noted that 'thirteen times a day Israelis stop whatever else they are doing to learn whether there has been some crippling new act of terror by their Arab enemies'.‡

Some correspondents were convinced that Israeli counteraction often had no appreciable effect, especially air-harassment of fedayeen camps. 'Of particularly questionable effect are the air raids on commando bases. These bases have only the flimsiest physical substance. The men scatter to their slit trenches while the planes at best knock down some shacks and tents which can be set up anew elsewhere tomorrow.'§ This was precisely the effect the Israelis wanted; 'retired' fedayeen have told me how unnerving it was to find that the Israeli airmen 'always seemed to know where to find us'.

An American reported that 'Fatah has restored pride, dignity and a sense of identity to the homeless Palestinians', and this was true enough. He quoted Abu Samra, a college-educated guerrilla leader. 'We are still fighting from a magic carpet but now on the West Bank of the Jordan we have a population in which we can swim like fish.'‖

* Patrick Marnham, *Daily Telegraph* magazine, February 28, 1969.
† *Observer*, May 8, 1969.
‡ H. A. Ruskin, *New York Times*, July 7, 1969.
§ Dana Adams Schmidt, *New York Times*, June 7, 1969.
‖ Bill Wise, *Life*, January 20, 1970.

116

But this was not true. Fedayeen saboteurs were taking food supplies with them into the occupied zone, knowing the reluctance of the local Palestinians to feed them and the readiness with which they betrayed fedayeen groups.

During the years 1968-70 the French Press—from *Le Monde* to the Communist *l'Humanité*—promoted the idea that Fatah was the only force on the Arab side. In order to do so they used the methods of international dramatisation and exaggeration, the portrayal of tendencies as facts, ignoring those groups in the neighbouring countries and the occupied territories that were still powerful. The French thesis also appealed to many leftist circles who were not comfortable in the past when they had to support reactionary and dictatorial states against democratic Israel. Now they could encourage and support the 'revolutionary guerrilla movement' and find in it virtues it did not possess and that had been arbitrarily taken from the Algerian or Vietnamese wars of liberation.

Courted by world Press, Arafat, and later Habash, Hawatmeh and others, were ready with historical parallels. 'As Napoleon and Hitler were drowned in the snows of Russia, the sands of our deserts will swallow the Israelis,' Arafat told Gavin Scott.* But sometimes a reporter saw through the bravado, as did John Mecklin when he labelled Fatah 'a posturing, rag-tag lot'.† Arafat, as the leader of 'the third force in the Middle East', was now getting onto the covers of the world's magazines, winning publicity that no amount of Kuwaiti oil money could buy. The mass hijacking of Western aircraft brought even more publicity.

Then, with the war in Jordan, reality asserted itself. The surprise of the world over the near-liquidation of the Palestinians' military structure resulted from the disproportion between the fedayeen's psychological, social and military image and their actual character as human beings and fighters. A cartoonist expressed this disproportion in a cartoon depicting

* *Time*, March 30, 1970.   † *Fortune*, June 1970.

117

the world press and the 'New Left' blowing up a balloon bearing the face of Arafat.

The *Economist* (October 10, 1970) was one of the first responsible journals to reappraise the fedayeen after the war in Jordan: 'The trouble is that one casualty of the civil war has been the credibility of the guerrillas' spokesmen. The final toll of killed and wounded is unlikely to be more than one-tenth of the 30,000 they claimed. The majority of the inhabitants of the refugee camps managed to get out before the heavy fighting started. But it was by using the charge of "genocide", which was swallowed whole by President Numeiry of Sudan and in part by a lot of other people that the guerrillas saved themselves from total defeat.'

Even now Arafat seems not to have learned that journalists and commentators are suspicious of politicians who change their views as they change their interviewers. Within one week Arafat gave two outlines of Fatah's aims. In *Time*, December 21, 1970: 'A democratic, non-Zionist, secular state where we could all live in peace and equality as we did for thousands of years.... If the Zionists would accept this principle we could share power on a democratic basis. We would not insist on having an Arab majority'; and in *Al-Hayat*, Beirut, December 25, 1970: 'The liberation of Palestine and putting an end to Zionist penetration, political, economic, military and propaganda, into Moslem states—is one of the duties of the Moslem world. We must fight a Holy War against the Zionist enemy, who covets not only Palestine but the whole Arab region, including its holy places.'

By 1972 the media was self-critical about its approach to the fedayeen movement. Louis Rukeyser who conducts a daily programme, *Rukeyser's World*, on American Information Radio Network, said on March 14:

'American news coverage of the Arab guerrillas in recent years has resembled nothing so much as American news coverage of the Black Panthers—and in neither case has my profession covered itself with journalistic glory. With both groups there was a fascination with the reality and threat of violence. With both there was a tendency to over-rate their influence and to take with grave seriousness the most nonsensical extremes of rhetoric.

'In the case of the guerrillas, this resulted in some rather extensive news coverage aimed at perpetuating the notion that these militants now had the central role in determining the future of the Middle East. In fact, this has never been true—as is increasingly becoming clear.

'In my own travels in the area, including visits to nearly all the countries even remotely involved, I became convinced early on that war in the Middle East would remain inevit-able as long as two basic conditions continued—first, an Arab unwillingness genuinely to accept the permanence of Israel, and second, a determination by the Soviet Union to egg the Arabs on and supply them with the necessary armaments. All else is secondary. The guerrillas, far from being the dominant force in the region, in reality have been shut off and turned on like a propaganda spigot by the Arab governments that border Israel. . . . Neither Lebanon nor Syria showed much appetite for the conflict these guerrillas plainly hoped to provoke. [Syria has since become more aggressive.]

'And since Israel already has effectively neutralized most of the guerrillas in Jordan and the Gaza Strip, their potency anywhere in the area is at a low ebb. This doesn't mean that there will never be another incident; it does mean that Mid-east peace depends more than ever not on the hot oratory of a colorful guerrilla but on the cold decisions of the Kremlin.'

Rukeyser's assessment finally put the whole relationship be-tween fedayeen and media into perspective. But the media must carry some of the blame for fedayeen shame; the Palestinians simply cannot live up to the reputation created for them.

12 *Israeli Mastery*

Israel's techniques and methods in countering fedayeen activity, at first hesitant and experimental, have reached a high degree of sophistication and effectiveness. Basically, the Israelis have depended on massive and sometimes harsh, reprisals, sophisticated interrogation techniques, enlightened administration in the occupied areas, bluff, technological developments and a superb intelligence service.

By 1972 the Israelis had so completely mastered the 'terrorist problem' within Israel and across its borders that it was difficult to believe that the fedayeen movement had been a serious problem a few years before. As late as June 1969 Elie Landau, a leading Israeli military writer, wrote: 'The fighting with Fatah goes on violently every day. This is never mentioned in the news.... Despite severe casualties, they [the guerrillas] keep mounting operations as though nothing has happened.... [At night] tens of terrorist bands acting on all fronts force us ... to exert increasing defence efforts.'*

With the terrorists as active as this it is all the more remarkable that within two years the Israelis had almost eliminated terrorist operations—except in Gaza—with the undoubted help of King Hussein.

Arab writers tend to oversimplify Israeli counter-fedayeen techniques and methods. Dr. Sharabi has written: 'In its efforts to crush the resistance, Israel adhered to a classic policy of

* *Maariv*, June 9, 1969.

pacification. In its basic structure, this policy most resembles the pacification policy of the French in Algeria, i.e. maintaining the status quo through a system of severe punishment alternating with limited concessions and rewards; and, as in Algeria, the pacification of occupied territory has led to increasing dependence on coercion and repression.' Sharabi's statement could only be based on second-hand evidence, since he himself had not been in Israel since 1948. Coercion and repression are such positive and aggressive acts that they should be apparent but it is almost impossible to see any signs of either. Indeed, the Israelis know very well that coercion and repression breeds resistance so they practise neither.

Sharabi speaks of Israel's 'basic strategic principle of always waging war on Arab soil, never on its own'. This is sophistry. Militarily the principle he refers to is a sound one and has been held as an ideal by all military leaders since conflict began. But Israel was no more able to adhere to its principle than most other belligerents; all three of its wars have involved fighting on part of its own soil. In any case, the fedayeen have been waging war on Israeli soil since 1965.

Israel has a reputation for making pre-emptive strikes, the classic example being the Six-Day War. But a reputation for reprisal strikes would be more justifiable, for Israel has rarely made a raid to abort or pre-empt an enemy attack. Indeed, when the fedayeen began to make their first stings the Israeli authorities faced an interesting dilemma. By not replying in kind to Arab incursions they might further encourage the fedayeen; but to reply in kind could build up Fatah in the eyes of the Arabs.

For nearly six months after Fatah had started its actions Israel held its forces down to ambushes and interception. The government felt goaded into retaliatory action but before any such action the Israeli authorities used to publish their justification, naming Fatah's operations and virtually revealing where the reprisal would take place. This was a mistake, for it was

121

tantamount to high commendation of Fatah, whose leaders could then boast to the Arab states that the Palestinian fedayeen had found the magic formula by which Israel could be fought. The propaganda and publicity had its effect: Fatah's example of inflicting damage on the enemy could only arouse applause by the Arab public, thus criticism of Fatah was equivalent to defending Israel.

In October 1966 two incidents in the Jerusalem area which the Israelis believed to have been carried out by commandos based in Syria, caused anxiety and induced them to consider taking reprisals. At this time there were repeated acts of sabotage and shooting incidents along the Syrian border and the Security Council met at Israel's request to hear its charges against the Syrians; a resolution condemning Syria was vetoed by the Soviet Union.

In the early hours of November 13, shortly after the mining of a patrol vehicle near the Jordanian border in which three Israeli soldiers were killed and six wounded, Israeli troops crossed into Jordanian territory in force and raided the village of Samu, south of Hebron. Four thousand Israeli troops took part and for the first time in a raid of this sort tanks were used. Jordanian troops hurrying to the scene were ambushed and suffered heavily. The Israelis withdrew after four hours having killed 18 Jordanians, wounded 134 and destroyed 127 buildings. The Israelis claimed that Samu had harboured terrorists coming originally from Syria. This was to set the pattern for the policy of retaliation, which reached its peak at Beirut Airport and the blowing up of Arab aircraft, and which has continued by land, sea and air ever since. The instant-reprisal method from the air—with the help of efficient Intelligence reports—destroyed many sabotage units. Israeli planes kept saboteurs constantly on the move as they sought new hiding places. Fear of quick retaliation forced many sabotage units to use delayed action devices; they could then bolt even before the bazooka or Katyusha rocket fired its charge.

I have seen a fedayeen document of September 17, 1969, signed by Fiyad Raga Sleiman, the acting commander of an area near Mount Hermon, asking his superior to transfer 21 named fedayeen 'because of fear and nervous breakdown caused by Israeli bombing of their bases'.

In 1968 the Israelis perfected another technique—that of searching towns in the West Bank—in what was known as 'Operation Ring' in Nablus. Surrounding the casbah at 3 a.m. on February 13 the Israelis picked up all the males and put them into compounds for scrutiny by Arab informers. The operation had been thought through to the last detail and was successful beyond expectation. Lunch was served for the thousands of people in the compounds. Two arms caches were found and 74 people were identified as belonging to terrorist organisations. In spite of this operation not all terrorists in the casbah were caught. A week later a group of saboteurs was trapped red-handed. They had been in the casbah throughout the search and had simply kept a step ahead of the searchers, moving from apartment to apartment through the passages concealed by wall cabinets and cupboard doors.

Most captured fedayeen readily talk, a statement which makes it necessary to examine the frequent charges of torture brought against the Israelis. I believe that some Israeli officials are capable of inflicting torture and would probably apply it— if it were necessary. In fact, it is not necessary because Arab prisoners can be easily induced to talk without resort to cruelty. Most of the tortures fedayeen prisoners complain about are nothing more than the tough questioning practised by security police in many countries and infinitely less cruel than methods used by some régimes.

Many independent observers, including experienced journalists who are not easily deceived by officialdom, have investigated allegations of torture. One Fatah accusation reached the United Nations.* It concerned Taysir Nabulsi, who told

* UN communiqué, HR 505, Amman, April 17, 1970.

the UN Commission he had been in charge of education in Jenin and that when the town was taken over in 1967 he was arrested and gaoled. Here, he testified, he was severely beaten, several of his teeth were knocked out, some fingernails were torn off and he was repeatedly given electric shocks. It transpired, however, that Nabulsi helped organise pupils' strikes so the military governor expelled him to Jordan. He never did see the inside of an Israeli prison.

Journalist David Pryce-Jones exhaustively investigated charges of torture in the occupied territories and reported that he could substantiate none of them. His account of an experience in Kalkilya is typical. The mayor's secretary, a young man held for three weeks, claimed that he had been beaten. Pryce-Jones wrote: 'He rolls up his trouser-leg to show me a scar on his shin about the size of sixpence. If this was from an Israeli kick, I ask, why is the scar-tissue the same brown colour as the rest of his leg? It should be new, pink. He shrugs. It is the first of dozens of such encounters.'*

David Caute had a similar experience. 'Virtually every Arab one meets alleges that prisoners are tortured in interrogation centres.... Personally I came up with no conclusive evidence. The Arab preference for allegation to evidence does not help the investigator. When I asked the mayor of Nablus and his colleagues to substantiate their charges by taking me to talk to any young Arab of the town who had been tortured they reverted to Arabic and then insisted it was the occupation, not its manifestations, which was intolerable. No doubt the Arabs are partly governed by their imaginations.'†

Ibrahim Al-Abid of the PLO Research Centre, Beirut, told me that he had proof of 'atrocities and murders' but he did not produce this proof. Much 'proof' is designed for more impressionable minds than those of professional researchers. All the Palestinian organisations have produced books of

* *Sunday Telegraph*, December 21, 1969.
† *Guardian*, April 26, 1970.

atrocity pictures, most of which are obviously faked or mis-interpreted or lacking in authentication. This has done great harm to the Palestinian cause for it raises doubts about the truth of all similar claims. 'Proof' has become an end in itself; the inquirer is supposed to accept it in lieu of evidence. Of all the Palestinians I have interviewed about allegations of torture I am inclined to believe only one, Faisal T. Musmar, a lecturer at the Teachers' Training College, Ramallah. He told me that he had been left hanging by his wrists from a hook during interrogation.

The Very Reverend George Appleton, Anglican Archbishop in Jerusalem, does not believe that torture is used in Israeli prisons or interrogation centres; this is an interesting viewpoint because the Israelis consider the archbishop an Arab sympathiser.*

For several reasons a feda'i prisoner talks readily—because he expects better treatment; because he wants credit for what he has done; because he believes that Israelis know everything already (they often don't) and because he is not prepared to accept punishment while a comrade is escaping—so he betrays him. Also, he is easily tricked. The Israelis once picked up a man they suspected of being a terrorist but all they *knew* about him was that he had a scar on his leg. During interrogation the Israeli Intelligence Officer brought out this information and the prisoner was so startled by this apparent omniscience that he quickly revealed all he knew. Another simple Israeli technique is to create suspicion. Interrogating officers will arrange a situation which suggests to one prisoner that another has given him away; his resentment will lead him into betraying himself and others though this will not stop him from posing as a national hero at his trial.

The policy in the occupied areas of blowing up houses whose owners have harboured fedayeen has been widely criticised

* The Arabs believe he is a 'Jew-lover'. In fact, the Archbishop is neutral and quite clearly is interested only in a peaceful settlement.

but has been highly effective. Such houses are, of course, cleared of people and property; there is no threat to life. The Israeli army takes great pains to ensure that innocent villagers are not hurt and that houses are only destroyed after 'conclusive evidence' that fedayeen have occupied them. Even so, mistakes have been made and houses wrongly destroyed. Compensation has been paid in such cases. Brigadier General Shlomo Gazit, the principal administrator, has said, 'We are very careful in making decisions and there is a rather complicated procedure in approving the blowing up of a house. Every single house, before being blown up, has to be approved by the Minister of Defence in person. And he does it only after seeing the file of the person involved. Wherever there is the least doubt—for example if the man is not in our hands or is in prison but has not admitted his guilt—the house is not blown up.'

The type of operations normally associated with guerrilla activity—attacks on police stations, barracks and transport— have never developed in Israel, so most counter-fedayeen activities *inside* Israel proper are nothing more than standard procedure. Everyone must carry identity papers; vehicles licensed to Arabs from the administered areas have different coloured plates. Israeli Arabs are not restricted in travel but there are many and varied checkpoints. Weapons and explosives are extremely difficult for Arabs to get; continuous efforts are made to discover and confiscate any held by Arabs and there is surveillance on secret radio communication.

A fedayeen cell is quickly detected, often through informers. Once a single arrest is made the whole cell usually blows. Early in 1970 the entire 37 members of a group operating in Hebron were taken within a few days. It had been responsible for several ambush murders, including the deaths of two American tourists. Hazim al-Khalidi, an expert and dispassionate Arab observer of the scene from the vantage point of his home in East Jerusalem, considers that 95 per cent of the fedayeen who are captured are given away by their own people.

The low point of Israeli morale occurred in May 1970—when 43 soldiers and 18 civilians were killed, 105 soldiers and 31 civilians wounded by fedayeen and Arab regular military action—and coincided with the creation of a virtually impenetrable curtain of defences from just south of the Sea of Galilee to the 'lido' near the Dead Sea and then on further into the Arava. More than half the Israelis' anti-fedayeen effort is in keeping their enemies beyond the borders separate from their potential enemies inside. They are greatly aided by the post-1967 boundaries being so much shorter—330 miles against 600 miles pre-war.

The principal deterrent is parallel barbed-wire fences enclosing wide minefields and liberally sprinkled with electronic warning devices and booby traps. At strategic points along the valley are forts capable of holding out for months of siege. At certain crossing places are fields of phosphorescent sand which sticks to the feet of saboteurs and makes them easy to trail. The Israelis sweep dust roads with barbed-wire or cloth to facilitate detection of tracks and they use searchlights, helicopters, dogs, and Bedouin tribal trackers. The fedayeen themselves believe that at many points machine guns operate automatically by infra-red rays. Such devices do exist in Europe but it is immaterial whether the Israelis have them or not; it is sufficient that the fedayeen believe in their existence. The more dangerous sections of the front are guarded by regulars, while the softer zones are covered by reserves doing their thirty days of annual combat duty.

More specifically, the 110-mile desert line from Eilat to the Dead Sea is secured by an inter-connected system of reconnaissance from the air, mechanised ground patrols and constantly changing observation posts equipped with the latest scientific detection devices. Security is based on mobile strength being immediately available. The 50-mile Dead Sea boundary is easily secured by the sea itself, a road and cliffs along the western bank and radar devices. The 60 miles from the Dead Sea to the Sea of Galilee are progressively easier to cross as the Jordan itself is not a real military obstacle most of the year. The Israelis hold the Jordan line with a lot of barbed-wire, minefields, radar, other detection devices and patrols. It is virtually impossible for a fedayeen patrol to cross this border and get far enough into the Israeli side during a single night to be among friendly Palestinians.

North-east of the Jordan River the 55-mile border follows the narrow valley of El Hama or Yarmuk. The first 20 miles of this border are between Israel and Jordan; the rest, to Mount Hermon, is between Israel and Syria. Much of the country is rugged with ideal positions for snipers. Across the Syrian Plain towards the Golan Heights the Israelis have no barrier that is proof against determined infiltrators but they have the great advantage that the Syrian Arabs who lived in this area fled to Syria in 1967. The native Druze people stayed. They worked out satisfactory relations with the Israelis, then asked for and were given full citizenship, with all the obligations and privileges that go with it. Aggressive by nature and accurate with weapons, the Druze are avoided by the fedayeen infiltrators.

During 1971 and early 1972 the Syrian Government fostered more than a hundred attempts by fedayeen groups, principally from Sa'ika and Fatah, to penetrate the Israeli defences along the Israel–Syrian border. This hilly region, mostly wooded, is well suited to guerrilla activity, but not one group got through and most suffered casualties. For the first time in many years the eleven Israeli agricultural settlements in the Golan Heights have been able to work without hindrance.

The Israeli Army rarely presents profitable targets for the fedayeen; the border posts are held by platoons with no vast stores of ammunition or fuel to be blown up. Most armoured vehicles are either dug in or kept behind ridges ready to be rushed to crisis points. All are moved about frequently. The Palestinians are poor shots and many cannot hit a stationary bus at 400 yards; most Israeli soldiers walk upright within sniper range and those in trucks or half-tracks calmly sit upright. Even a sniper gets heavy return fire, sometimes from tank guns and mortars. An investigator for the American business magazine *Fortune* found that in the earlier part of 1970 fedayeen groups were losing up to 80 per cent of the men committed to an attack.* The fedayeen generally admit to greater casualties than the Israelis claim to have inflicted.

Between June 1967 and the end of 1971 the Israel Defence Forces carried out 5,270 operations across the cease-fire line; nearly 1,400 of these were in the air, another 100 were at sea and the rest were army operations. The official military spokesman announced only 577 of the operations.†

One highly effective Israeli measure has been the development of nahal settlements along the frontiers. A nahal is a military formation which combines military tasks with agriculture and, more recently, with some industry. The function of nahal 'forts' is identical with that of the forts the Romans and Byzantines set up along their frontiers, but a nahal village is not a fort in strict military parlance, though it may be surrounded by barbed-wire and defended by fortified positions. The young people who live in them are not regular soldiers but volunteers. The roots of the nahalim are in the Palmach, the Israeli army formed before the partition, when the Hagana was looking for a way to train members on a fulltime basis in an inconspicuous way. Some nahal members would normally be disqualified from the army because of police records or because they have had too little formal education. In a nahal these young men and women have developed great self-respect and *esprit de corps*. Once an area is considered safe a nahal settlement becomes a regular kibbutz and by 1972 more than

* John M. Mecklin, *Fortune*, June 1970.
† Figures given by General Bar-Lev, former Israeli Chief of Staff; quoted in *The Jerusalem Post*, January 1, 1972.

twenty nahalim had been turned over to fulltime farmers; another thirty settlements may have been abandoned had not nahal men and women taken over from earlier settlers who, while not defeated, were too dispirited by Arab enmity.*

A powerful weapon in the Israeli counter-fedayeen armoury is the Arabs' belief that Israeli technological wizardry is unbeatable. Several educated Palestinians, including Ibrahim Al-Abid, have told me that the Israelis feed into highly sophisticated computers all the utterances of fedayeen leaders and can then predict the enemy plans. Since June 1969 attempts by other Palestinian leaders to put the Israeli Intelligence Services in perspective have had little success.†

Israel's success in preserving its borders against enemy penetration and preventing Israeli Arabs from gaining sufficient experience and organisation to become really dangerous has led to the frustrating in the Israel–Arab confrontation of perhaps the most important fedayeen advantage in other parts of the world—the creation of an image of inevitable victory.

There is no feeling in Israel of inevitable defeat, even if there is one of incessant conflict. In a Hebrew song a young draftee tells his girl: 'Whenever we stroll we are three—you, I and the next war.... When we smile in a minute of love, the next war smiles with us.' This illustrates the matter-of-fact acceptance by young Israelis of their national predicament. They have learned that their foes will make no concessions and they believe now, after several bouts of false optimism, that the conflict will be protracted. Throughout Israel young Israelis

---

* But many stayed. As one example, the kibbutz Kfar Ruppin extends to the edge of the Jordan; on the far bank, less than a hundred feet away, is Jordanian, and for years, fedayeen territory. Kfar Ruppin was continually pounded by rockets and mortar shells and the children slept for a long time in underground shelters. Yet only two of the 350 kibbutz members left because of the attacks.

† 'I can affirm from experience and with total responsibility that the rumours about the strength of the Israeli Intelligence Services is a myth. Israel is not particularly advanced in its Intelligence as such.' Abu Ayad, a member of Fatah's Central Committee, in an interview with Lutfi al-Khouli, editor-in-chief of the Egyptian monthly, *Al-Tali'ah*, June 1969.

have a general sympathy for the Palestinian refugees, largely because they see them as 'pathetic' political pawns.

Whatever the Palestinian Arabs—the fedayeen—claim about the ineffectiveness of Israeli counter-measures, whatever they allege against the Israelis, one truth is self-evident: they conspicuously and disastrously lack a base inside the occupied territories. There could be no more conclusive proof that, as a guerrilla movement, the fedayeen have failed. Such failure was foreseen by the British military writer, Brigadier Peter Young, in March 1968.

At present guerrilla warfare seems attractive to the Arab activists. It is a natural reaction on the part of nations which, though beaten in the field, wish to continue the struggle. The comparison with the resistance movements of the Second World War will be obvious. In my view, guerrilla warfare will get the Arabs nowhere, not because of Israel's reprisal raids ... but because the Arabs have no real talent for commando-style operations. The fact that T. E. Lawrence used the Bedouin for raids against the Turks proves nothing, since his style of operation would be quite impossible against aircraft and armour. More to the point, the Israelis with their experience of subversive war against the British, know exactly what they are up against, and are able to put down any fifth column among their Arab population....*

It would be easy to suppose from Israeli military success, and indeed it is sometimes stated, that Israel is among the most aggressive of nations. By force of circumstance, perhaps, but not by nature. Israel is unwarlike, and that it is a symbol of military valour in the Middle East, where the traditionally warrior Arab society suffers defeat after defeat, is one of the strangest ironies of history.

* Quoted by the *Jewish Chronicle*, London, March 29, 1968.

13 *'The High Summer has passed'*

The strategic thinking of fedayeen leaders in 1970 was based on these fundamental assumptions:

1. That the Egyptian front would remain firm or, better still, that the Egyptians would attack.
2. That the Egyptian, Jordanian, Syrian and Iraqi forces would continue to improve in equipment and military effectiveness.
3. That increasing Arab strength and co-ordination would overtake Israel's military superiority.
4. That a defensive war of attrition would steadily escalate and cause Israel increasingly severe losses.
5. That Israel's control of the occupied territories would become increasingly severe, leading to total repression and terror.

By mid-1971 not one of these expectations was confirmed so that the whole fedayeen movement was in a state of such obvious decline that foreign observers were no longer qualifying their opinions about its ineffectiveness. A Canadian saw that 'the high summer of the Palestine Liberation Organisation has passed and there is little chance of its ever blooming again. The Arab guerrilla movement is dying a slow, kicking death.'*

From the objective political distance of Norway a leading journalist decided that the movement was finished 'because it

---

* Derek Maitland, *Toronto Star*, June 25, 1971.

wanted to do so many things at the same time—to fight against Israel; to fight against "reactionary" Arab régimes; to fight against "progressive" Arab régimes wanting some kind of peace with Israel.... A bitter lesson it must have been to see, when the tragedy was fulfilled in the Jordan Valley, that many guerrillas preferred to surrender to the one who all the time was proclaimed as its main enemy, the Israelis. It was evident that many preferred Israeli prisons to King Hussein's platoons.'*

Early in 1971 a single denigrating remark about the terrorists in an Arab newspaper was considered an act of treachery. A few months later criticism of Fatah was open and unrestrained. Arab writers were disillusioned by lack of fedayeen accomplishment, the depth of their despair reflecting the height of their former hopes. The Palestinian journalist, Nabil Khury, wrote:

The answer [to the Palestinian problem] lay in the 'hopes' of the resistance and its success but today, after the mistakes of the resistance, due to the inability of the leadership to reach the required standard, and after the slaughter—it suffered daily. The hope in all its aspects has flickered and spluttered out. We do not want to be a part of Israel.... We feel that all the Arab states cannot now force Israel to accept any solution, whether of peace or war. We feel that all these states are in a plot against us and our future. Therefore, only one solution is left to us, which is that we say 'Yes!' to a Palestinian State. We have no choice but to agree to a state like this. This is the choice we prefer to returning to a dictatorial, oppressive and reactionary rule.†

Egyptian reaction was more poetic but no less fundamental. 'The Palestine guerrilla can now be compared to a string of

* Karl Emil Hagelund, *Dagbladet*, Oslo, July 24, 1971.
† Nabil Khury, *Al-Hawadess*, Beirut, April 23, 1971.

pearls fallen apart, with pearls scattered in all directions without control....'*

Long before King Hussein's first crushing of the fedayeen in October 1970 other Arab governments were looking warily at the organisations' intentions. PLO spokesmen were touring the world and making statements which could only fill Arab régimes with suspicion and foreboding. One of the most influential of Palestinian intellectuals, Dr. Yusif Sayegh, lecturing in London, warned that 'soon the Palestinian liberation movement and revolution will be transformed into an Arab movement and revolution ... and the Arab governments will all have to hammer out their policies and their actions in harmony with the requirements of the war of liberation.'†

But Arab governments do not want their countries involved in revolution and they do not want to be forced to hammer out policies at the whim of the Palestinian Arabs.

By July 1971 even the Syrians were looking suspiciously at the fedayeen. A large cargo of Chinese arms for Fatah arrived at the Syrian port of Latakia. The consignment included tanks, transport vehicles and a rich supply of light arms and ammunition. The local military governor reported at once to the Syrian Chief of Staff; he conferred with President Assad, who ordered the cargo to be locked up. Assad is reported to have asked Arafat, 'What do you want with all this equipment? Do you want to occupy Syria? Not even the Syrian army has such tanks.' Arafat said that the arms were for the so-called Yarmuk Brigade, which consisted then of 6,000 men. Assad refused to release the arms because, according to Arafat, the Syrians did not want to insult the Russians. But principally, Assad feared that Fatah might become too strong, as it had in Jordan.

By October 1971 the fedayeen organisations were interfering

---

* Mohammed Heikal, *Al-Ahram*, July 2, 1971.

† April 15, 1970, Central Hall, Westminster; under the sponsorship of the Council for the Advancement of Arab–British Understanding.

in Tunisian affairs by calling for the overthrow of what they term 'the fascist régime' of President Bourguiba. A joint statement signed by all major groups charged the Tunisian government with masterminding the assassination in Beirut of the Arab Liberation Front's leader, Ibrahim Sukeimi. The statement said that 'The criminals will be punished with the fall of the fascist régime and the victory of the popular forces.'

The Arab governments cannot decide what the terrorist movement really is and what its role should be. Is it a resistance intended to bridge the military gap between two conventional wars against Israel? Is it a supporting force in a war of attrition? Is it the nucleus of a nationalistic movement on its way to a long-range guerrilla war—that is, within the Arab nations? All Arab nations uphold the 'Palestinian Revolution' in principle and reject it in practice. Saudi Arabia supported the fedayeen for as long as they refrained from blowing up oil pipelines. Iraq supports them as long as they do not try to 'corrupt' Iraqi students; Syria offers support provided the fedayeen keep the Syrian border calm; Jordan, much weaker, tolerated them until they threatened national security; Lebanon, weaker still, has had to screw up its courage and insist that the fedayeen do nothing to provoke Israeli counter-measures.

The Libyan ruler, Colonel Ghadafi, has criticised the fedayeen for their 'paltry achievements' and has urged them to turn their war into an internal one. 'We do not consider the members of PFLP and the Popular Democratic Front as fighters or liberators. They are not fedayeen. They are really agents. They are advocates of division and theories and not advocates of armed struggle.... The groups led by George Habash and Nayef Hawatmeh have no principles....'*

Nevertheless, Libya supports the fedayeen with men, arms and money and Ghadafi announced that he would not join the Federation of Arab Republics if Egypt executed the four terrorists accused of the assassination of the Jordanian Prime

* Libyan Radio, August 1, 1971, reported by BBC Monitoring Service.

Minister, Wasfi el-Tel, in Cairo. They were subsequently released 'on bail', though it is unlikely that they will ever stand trial. Despite his criticisms of the Maoist and Trotskyist elements in the fedayeen movement, Ghadafi is a fiery supporter of all action against Israel. He has sent Libyans to serve in Fatah, and at Libyan naval bases trains Palestinian fedayeen in naval warfare and marine sabotage. After the Munich massacre it was left to Ghadafi to offer Arab burial to the terrorists killed in the final shooting. It was he too who gave sanctuary to the three surviving terrorists after they were exchanged for a Lufthansa airliner hijacked by members of the Black September gang. Ghadafi must appear to the Israelis a considerable threat in encouraging fedayeen activity.

After their expulsion from Jordan and conscious of their ineffectiveness against Israel, Palestinians began to indulge in 'group-think' or a form of group therapy. I have listened to numerous interminable rehashings of the old problems with never a new idea or expression forthcoming. Every senior fedayeen leader I have met is neurotic and apprehensive, given to fits of profound despair, acutely sensitive to the slightest criticism from anywhere in the Arab world and worried about the possibility of a political settlement.

Sharabi believes that a political settlement imposed or supported by the great powers of the United States, the Soviet Union, France and Britain 'probably constitutes the greatest threat to the Palestine guerrilla movement. It would bring about the immediate tranquillization of the situation and simultaneously the creation of an environment fundamentally inimical to the growth of guerrilla power.'

One serious fedayeen problem has been the gulf between ambitions and the impracticability of attaining them. Nowhere has this been better shown than in a statement by the PLO leader Dr. Nabil Sh'at when he attended a Palestinian convention in Kuwait in April 1971. He was asked his opinion of the 'problem' of Arab employment in Israel and of the handicap this must be to the future of the resistance movement on the West Bank. 'This is truly a great problem,' Dr. Sh'at said, 'we cannot ask the Arab workers to desist from working in Israel for that is asking them to die of hunger. Secondly, to force them to cross to the East Bank is a thing which is not according to our wishes in any form, for this falls in with Israeli planning.... At the same time we cannot escape from or forget the danger resulting from their working in and their contact with Israel. *In my opinion, the solution is escalation of resistance within the entire Bank to convert it into a second Gaza, and then the problem will solve itself* [my italics].'*

Failure forced Fatah into a drastic reappraisal in 1971, the major decision being to end bureaucracy, partly by closing its offices in Lebanon. The organisation also announced its intention to maintain 'secrecy of status as well as of operation'. A spokesman said that Fatah's 'overvisibility' had been exploited by the movement's enemies.

Leaders were able to use the comments of foreign sympathisers to rationalise their 'new philosophy'. A favourite statement is one by the English Middle East specialist John Reddaway:

The idea that the Palestinian Resistance would ever be capable of developing into an army of liberation was always a chimaera and has been at the root of many of the difficulties and disappointments besetting the guerrillas. It has also encouraged a comfortable delusion among other Arabs that they could now opt out of the struggle against Israel and leave it to the Palestinians. A strategy for a long haul against Israel must include reshaping and streamlining the Resistance Movement for the limited tasks which are all it can properly be expected to undertake—those of forcing the Palestine grievance on to the attention of the world and of harassing the authorities in Israel to the point where

* Quoted by Nabil Khury in *Al-Hawadess*, Beirut, April 23, 1971. Khury comments: 'Dr. Sh'at forgot to tell how.'

they must constantly be asking themselves whether it would not be better for them to come to terms.*

On-the-spot observers see the Palestinian plight in a quite different light: 'The masses cannot be mobilised by a mere appeal to fight Israel; they suffer exploitation not at the hands of the Zionists but rather at the hands of the Arab ruling classes. It is these classes, too, who since 1948 have oppressed the people of Palestine. They have kept them outside the productive process, penned them up in camps, living on the charity of big powers and everywhere subject to special regulations. They have used racism and chauvinism to set them apart from the other Arab people.'† This viewpoint is supported by much evidence. The Libyan Prime Minister, Abdel Salem Jalloud, has said that the Arabs have kept the Palestinian refugees in tents according to a planned policy for the return of Palestine; the rehabilitation of the Palestinians in Arab countries would have lost them Palestine for good.‡

Many Palestinian refugees might have been kept in tents but the conflict with Israel has given Palestinian women their best opportunity to assert themselves as individuals and mount a 'revolution' of their own—storming the bastion of Arab-world male superiority. Leila Khaled achieved international notoriety and many others have become well known in Lebanon, Gaza and the West Bank. Mostly young and often educated in the West—France, England, the United States—the Palestinian girl fedayeen have a better political understanding than their male counterparts. Indeed, they are more the material from which real revolutionaries are made. Proportionate to their numbers they have caused the Israelis more trouble than have their male comrades.

* *Middle East International*, September 1971.
† Samir Franjieh, a journalist of the Beirut daily, *L'Orient-le Jour*, in *Journal of Palestine Studies*, Winter 1972.
‡ *El Havadat*, Beirut, January 5, 1972. Major Jalloud was not Prime Minister when he made this statement.

Fatmah Burnawi (Bernaoui), 23, was the first woman arrested for terrorist activities. A nurse in a hospital in the West Bank town of Kalkilya, Miss Burnawi was an underground member of Fatah as early as 1965. She was arrested for the attempted demolition of the Zion Cinema in Jerusalem. Miriam Shakhashir, 19, of Nablus was one of the group which planted bombs in the Hebrew University cafeteria; the Odeh sisters—Rasmia, 23, Laila, 21, and Aicha, 18, put bombs in a supermarket in Jerusalem; Aida Issa threw two bombs into a bank in Gaza.

Women were responsible for many of the demonstrations and students' strikes. During 1969-70 women and children became increasingly involved in revolutionary activity. Girls between the ages of 18 and 30 joined organisations as nurses, typists and teachers in Fatah-run schools. Some teenage girls took part in missions across the cease-fire lines. A young Palestinian woman dentist, Dr. Musmar, ran an underground medical clinic for wounded fedayeen in Nablus before she was betrayed and arrested. A group of girls from Ramallah sent poisoned chocolates to selected enemies.

Women other than Palestinians have been fairly easily recruited. Two Moroccan sisters admitted planning, with a German girl, to blow up hotels in Israel on Popular Front orders. The girls were said to have smuggled explosives into Israel in their brassières. In Rome, in August 1972, two fedayeen picked up two 18-year-old British girls and prepared them as carriers of a bomb to be taken on an El Al aircraft. After treating the girls to an 11-day life of luxury the Palestinians suggested that they all go to Israel and bought four tickets on an El Al flight. The men then said they could not make the trip on the day planned but urged the girls to go ahead; they would all meet later in Tel Aviv. As a 'present and a pledge of friendship' they insisted that the girls take a cassette player —which had been fitted with a bomb. Because El Al men refused to allow the player into the cabin and placed it in the reinforced hold, the explosion was not serious enough to destroy the plane, which landed safely.

An Arab girl pays a high price for fedayeen action. She loses face in the marriage market and has practically no hope of making a good marriage. In one case on the West Bank a dozen men of a family asked the Israeli military governor to blow up their houses rather than send a girl of the family to gaol. I have spoken at length to several fedayeen women, including some who have served periods in prison. Without exception they said they would repeat the act for which they were punished. Very few of the many male fedayeen I interviewed who had been in prison, were still in prison or had 'retired', would return to terrorist activities—or so they said. The difference in attitudes was startling.

Other women have turned into propagandists. One of the best known is Mrs. Walid Khalidi (wife of Professor Khalidi of the American University of Beirut, who is also Director of the Institute of Palestinian Studies). She does her part for the 'cause' by heading the Arab Women's Information Committee. This group, operating from the basement of Mrs. Khalidi's home in the Beirut suburb of Zarif, produces clumsy anti-Israel propaganda. Mrs. Khalidi, a sister of the Lebanese premier, believes that the fedayeen leaders realise that their cause is lost and that they would favour a political settlement, but dare not say as much; such an admission would ruin their career and endanger their lives.

Another prominent intellectual woman feda'i is Soraya Antonius, secretary of the Fifth of June Society in Beirut. Infinitely more practical and intelligent than the male Palestinian intellectuals, Miss Antonius has a dispassionate dedication to Palestinianism that should worry both the Israelis and the Arab leaders. 'We found that when we picked up a gun people wanted to talk with us,' she said. 'This had never happened before. It made us think. But it's silly to say that the Palestine problem is the problem of 80 million Arabs; not

nore than a few thousand Arabs care about Palestine.' It is
a safe assumption that the women among these few thousand
are among the most militant. As the advance guard of a
growing army of Arab women demanding equality with men
they could bring a genuine revolution to the Arab world.

UNRWA has put forward many projects aiming at the
rehabilitation of the Palestinian refugees by constructing permanent residence units. The Arabs regarded these projects as
having one aim—the liquidation of the Palestinian problem;
rehabilitation would mean the end of refugees and acceptance
of the state of Israel as a *fait accompli*. '... In order to counteract the rehabilitation projects the Palestinians launched general
strikes, mass demonstrations and destroyed many of the hous-
ing units set up by UNRWA. The rehabilitation projects were
presented by Dag Hammarskjöld in 1959 in the form of a plan
for the integration of the Palestinians in the economic life of
the Middle East.... The Arab governments opposed it, thus
forcing the UN to withdraw the plan.'*

For as long as UNRWA camps exist in their present form
they will remain hotbeds of intrigue and havens for violent
men. UNRWA is a form of insurance which allows fedayeen
to be active without real fear of Israeli observation and reprisal.
Ninety-nine per cent of UNRWA staff are themselves
Palestinian—a disproportionate number if UNRWA is to be
seen to be not politically involved in the Israel–Arab dispute.

The refugee camps, especially those in Lebanon, are still the
chief fedayeen recruiting grounds, shelters for saboteurs and
bases for every kind of revolutionary activity. Military training
sometimes takes place within the camps and all have their
own military police—men of the Armed Struggle Command—
at the gates. Under these men the camps are well disciplined.
Shukeiri had long cherished the dream of direct command over
the refugee camps; at the end of 1969 Fatah had realised this

* Leila S. Kadi, *Basic Political Documents of the Armed Palestinian Resistance Movement*, PLO Research Centre, Beirut, December 1969.

dream, with bases in all 30 refugee camps from Nahr el-Bard in northern Lebanon to the southern Jordanian desert. Some Israelis allege that a few UNRWA officials have threatened to withhold ration cards if certain men did not join fedayeen organisations, and that UNRWA trucks have been used to carry weapons and orders.

No matter how efficient the local leadership, no refugee camp is attractive. All are crowded and depressing places, hot and dusty in summer and cold and muddy in winter. However, life in the camps should be seen in some perspective. Many Palestinians are better off in refugee camps than they would be outside, though this does not imply that conditions are acceptable. The refugees have medical and dental care, and all children are given a sound education, though classes are too large and double-shifting is now common. The food ration is no more than barely adequate but UNRWA's resources are strained to the limit.

The great tragedy of the camps is their continued use as political weapons. The mass of the Palestinians in them are pawns in a struggle few of them understand.

14 *The Depths of Desperation*

All the fedayeen leaders have sought to explain the failure of the movement. George Habash sees the root of the evil in Arafat's hesitation, at least until March 1971, to test his strength in guerrilla warfare against the 'reactionary' Arab régimes which, especially in Jordan and Lebanon, placed obstacles in his path. Nayef Hawatmeh feels that the mistake was in entrusting the command of the Palestinian Revolution to the hands of 'bourgeois elements', like Arafat, who did not understand the value of class warfare within the context of the national struggle. The veteran professional officers of the 'Palestine Liberation Army' maintain that the terrorists marshalled their units contrary to all military logic and became needlessly entangled in battles in which they were at a disadvantage. And in defence the military leaders of Fatah believe that had the political commissars not been allowed to do as they pleased the movement would have gained another few years to strengthen and organise itself.

Abu Zuluf, editor of *Al-Quds*, the East Jerusalem daily, puts some of the blame on the fedayeen leaders for committing themselves to alignment with any régime—the Soviet Union, Egypt or Iraq; they should have remained entirely Palestinian.* Privately fedayeen leaders admit that they would like political talks with Israel, and are offended that the Israelis will not meet them. They do not realise that the fedayeen movement

* In an interview with the author, October 24, 1971.

143

must first fulfil three conditions, imposed not by Israel but by the dictates of politics. They are: (1) Israel must be convinced that the fedayeen movement's military potential is dangerous; (2) all the Palestinian organisations must be unified and show clearly that they are recognised by the population of the occupied territories and that they are truly representative of Palestinian opinion; (3) this unified organisation must show that it is trusted and supported by all Arab countries.

A direct Israeli condition would be that the fedayeen give up their principal objective—to put an end to the existence of Israel. Again, the Israelis would agree to talk only with somebody they could believe; they do not think the present leaders qualify. In justifying their point of view, Israelis point to an Arafat interview much quoted in fedayeen propaganda. Arafat was asked: 'The Zionists claim that Fatah and the Arabs are waging a war of extermination against the Jews, and in the event of their defeat they will be "thrown into the sea". How do you respond to this?'

Arafat's reply: 'Our aim is to bring an end to the concept of a Jewish Zionist state, a racist expansionist state. Our aim is to destroy this state, this concept—but not its people. We want a democratic Palestinian state. We will not force out anyone who is willing to live under the banner of this state as a loyal Palestinian. It does not matter whether he is Christian, Moslem or Jew.'*

The Israelis ask: 'How do you destroy a state without destroying the people who make up the state?'

Abu Lutf, a member of the Fatah Central Committee claims that the nature of Israeli society is artificial. 'How could these people who came from the west, others from the east, north and south, who spoke different languages and had different habits and nationalities, how could they possibly form a homogenous society in such a short period!' And then, uninten-

---

* Edmund Ghareeb, 'An Interview with Abu Ammar', *The Arab World*, May 1969.

ionally, he gives one answer to his own question: 'The Israelis are living under circumstances of continuous struggle with he Arab people.'*

There is nothing artificial about Israeli identity. It is made up, as the Israelis see it themselves, of 3,500 years of Jewish culture and history, the Hebrew language, Israel's social structures, and the way Israeli democracy works. On top of this the 'continuous struggle' Abu Lutf speaks of has given Israel a degree of solidarity, unity and cohesion the young state could otherwise have built only by the lengthy process of social evolution. The fedayeen attitude caused an important change in the attitude of many Israelis towards statehood; it acquired great value even for those for whom previously it was not a value. The conflict has also produced creativity. In Arab society the conflict has only been destructive.

The ordinary Israeli does not forget the deeds of fedayeen fighters; some have indeed been shocking in their brutality. One of the worst occurred on January 15, 1971, when terrorists killed a Druze tractor driver, Hussein Sharif Abu Hamad, while he was working in a field on the slopes of Mount Hermon. They decapitated him and took his head back to Lebanon. At a funeral in Abu Hamad's village the Israeli deputy prime minister appealed to the Lebanese authorities to 'perform a last act of grace for the murdered man's family and see that his head is returned to be buried with his body.' The PLO admitted to the killing but the head was not returned. A year later an engineer, Joseph Gruber, 24, of Haifa, was alone in a jeep on an early morning inspection tour of construction work near Golan Heights when terrorists attacked him. He was apparently shot at close range and the fedayeen then decapitated him and defiled the body. The head could not be found.

Such acts embitter Israelis and frustrate those Palestinians

* *Basic Political Documents of the Armed Palestinian Resistance Movement*, PLO Research Centre, Beirut, July 1969, p. 109.

who see that they delay any rapprochement. Many younger intellectual Palestinians, especially those who have travelled overseas, are no longer interested in conflict. In November 1971 a survey of the predominantly Moslem student body at the Université Libanaise, Beirut, showed that sixty per cent favoured a peaceful settlement to the Palestine problem. The Popular Front's paper, *Al-Hadaf*, edited by Ghassan Kanafani, bitterly criticised them. 'This poll reflects false convictions. . . . It proves that those who do not support fedayeen activity have expressed a capitalist, conservative and religious ideology.'

It may have expressed realism. I asked a young Palestinian-Lebanese with family connections in high Lebanese political circles for his opinion about the Palestine problem. He said, '*What* Palestine problem? There *is* no problem. The Jews live in Palestine in a state they call Israel. That's the end of it.'

The situation is not as simple as that, of course, although after mid-1971 the overall number of active fedayeen fell rapidly. Some men retired from revolutionary activities to become bodyguards for bar owners in Beirut, others are officials in the refugee camps. Many are now freely working in the occupied territories, and admit that they joined Fatah or one of the smaller groups for a job. One is a lonely, watchful boy named Abdullah Fayez Chemali whom I interviewed in a refugee camp near Hebron. Chemali had joined Fatah at the age of 17 to fight the Israelis—and found himself under fire from the Jordanians. He hid for a week and then, starving, chose the Israelis as the lesser of two evils. After four months in prison he found a job working on the roads. He told me he still respected his immediate leaders in Fatah but had no respect for Arafat, nor was he in any way grateful to the Israelis for giving him his life and a job. He frankly admitted he would join the fedayeen again 'when they become strong'.

Mohammed Housein Zaidat of the village of Beni Naim, near Hebron, joined Fatah because the only option was to join the Jordanian army—and Fatah paid him better. He surrendered and was briefly imprisoned before returning to his village, where his experiences made him more highly respected. He was still afraid of Fatah: 'They are bastards and will want revenge for my having surrendered to the Israelis.'

Revenge is a dominant theme in fedayeen thinking. All the organisations want revenge against Jordan, but a major threat to King Hussein will long remain the PFLP breakaway group of Wadi Haddad which, in April 1972, hijacked a Lufthansa airliner and ransomed it for £2,000,000. The profit was only £1,600,000 as the Government of South Yemen, to which the hijackers had taken the plane, wanted a £400,000 fee for allowing the Palestinians to leave the territory. This money was largely needed to finance operations against Jordan.

Revenge, and terrorism for its own sake, are two principal functions of Jihaz al-Rasd—usually known as Rasd—Fatah's underground organisation. Other roles are to gather military information about Israel, to counter espionage activities within Fatah, to screen recruits for Fatah and to guard leaders' lives. Its agents have murdered several Palestinians suspected of spying for Israel or for attempting to kill Arafat and others. Two of its members told me that they had eliminated Israeli agents from its ranks and that Rasd is able to get Israeli Intelligence to accept false information.

Rasd's early members were trained by the Egyptian Intelligence Service in 1969. The group's first leader was Mohammed Mustafa Shyein, also known as Salah Halef—the 'Abu Ayad' several times mentioned in this narrative. He was wounded, captured and executed in July 1971 after a fight between fedayeen and Jordanian troops. The best-known leader was Fuad Shemali, a Lebanese Christian who masterminded some of the earlier operations before he died of cancer in Geneva in August 1972. He left posthumous instructions to concentrate on kidnapping Israelis held in high esteem by Israelis themselves—scholars, scientists and athletes.

Shemali's successor was Mohammad Yusuf Najjar, known in fedayeen circles as Abu Yusuf, formerly a senior Rasd Intelligence officer. But the most feared leader is Ali Hassan Salamah (Abu Hassan) son of the famous Palestinian leader Sheikh Hassan Salamah, killed in a fight with the Israelis in 1948. Even Arafat is said to defer to Abu Hassan, who is apparently motivated by revenge for his father's death. His right-hand man is Ghazi el-Husseini, Rasd's technical expert. A German-educated engineer, he plans the operations formulated by Abu Hassan.

At this point it is difficult to find the line which divides Rasd from its 'special services section'—the Black September (*Ailul al-Aswad*) group. This group, the most violent manifestation of the Palestinians' frustration, came into being after the 'civil war' in Jordan, September 1970. It was long thought that its members were extremists who had no links with the major organisations, except perhaps Habash's PFLP. In fact, it is an integral part of Fatah and it receives its instructions from the Fatah leadership. By not officially recognising any connection, Fatah can carry out acts of terrorism without having to bear responsibility for them. Fatah's moderate approach pre-1970 and its apparent moderation after that time gained it a freedom of movement denied other Palestinian organisations with a less subtle approach.

Black September was directly controlled, in 1972, by Fakhri al-Amari, who led the team that killed Wasfi el-Tel. But real leadership is blurred and Abu Yusuf certainly had much authority. The group, in 1972, consisted of about 400 members —though US Intelligence sources said the figure was closer to 100. These men plan the operations, then recruit rank-and-file Fatah men to carry them out.

Most of Black September's actions were—and are likely to be—directed against Jordan and installations in Europe belonging to governments considered too friendly to Israel. In December 1971 the group made an abortive attempt on the life of the Jordanian Ambassador in London. In February 1972 another gang failed to hijack to Libya a Jordanian airliner flying from Cairo to Amman.

Rasd, and by association, Black September, are also connected with money-making; funds raised by Fatah are passed to Abu Hassan who transfers them to bank accounts in Switzerland, Italy and West Germany. They are then invested in business ventures—legitimate and otherwise—for high returns. The total investment in Europe is about £30 million.

Abu Hassan has set up a Rasd network in Europe, linked with the terrorist organisations such as the German Baader-Meinhoff group. He has recruited European left-wingers, many of them women; some have been trained by Fatah in Syria and lead various 'action cells' in France and Germany. Fatah had 23 branches in Germany in October 1972. Rasd will accept contracts to carry out operations unconnected with the Palestinian cause. One such contract was the explosion in March 1971 at the Gulf Oil Refinery, Rotterdam. A team of Europeans carried out the operation to Rasd's plans. Libya gave Rasd a contract to kidnap an exile living comfortably in Italy on funds allegedly amassed while serving ex-King Idris. When the Rasd team picked up this man he offered them double Libya's fee if they allowed him to escape to a friendly country. Rasd then reported to Libya that they could not locate the man. Rasd's extensive network is engaged in such lucrative enterprises as smuggling hashish. Lebanese members of the Black September group are involved in getting hashish into Europe and the operation has been so successful that half-kilo sacks are decorated with the picture of an Arab feda'i holding his sub-machine gun at the ready. Such commercial ventures are facilitated by the readiness of Algeria, Libya and the Sudan to provide diplomatic passports. Abu Hassan, for instance, has two Algerian passports in the names of Abdel Kadir Madani and Ahmed Belkacem. Fedayeen have access to Arab business offices in Europe, as well as embassies and consulates. The Algerian, Iraqi, Egyptian and South Yemen embassies are said to be especially helpful; the Libyans are also co-operative, particularly at their consulate in Geneva.

Black September's planners and operators are tougher and smarter than fedayeen of the past. They sent two men and two girls to hijack a Belgian airliner in May 1972. They forced it to land at Lod Airport and demanded the freedom of 308 terrorists held in Israeli prisons, on threat of blowing up the aircraft and its passengers. In an unprecedented commando operation the Israelis overcame the hijackers and saved the lives of passengers and crew. The two male hijackers were shot dead, the women captured.

The group's attempt to kidnap Israeli athletes at the Olympic Games in Munich and hold them as hostages against the release of 200 fedayeen held by the Israelis was as bold an action as any in the world history of terrorism. It was planned to create maximum outrage and it succeeded, probably beyond the planners' wildest dreams. The eight Palestinians involved exposed every weakness in the forces of law and in the helpless governments involved in the crisis. The failures of security, of crisis judgment and of police operations and information will be debated for years. Beyond that the fedayeen set off a widening wave of diplomatic, political, military and social consequences. But Black September's enterprise could be its downfall. The Munich operation was not the zenith of fedayeen activity but the nadir. It alienated world sympathy for the Palestinians' cause to a degree that no other action has done.*

The same desperation was evident in the letter bombs of September–October 1972. In all, 64 letter bombs were posted in Amsterdam and reached Israeli diplomatic offices in London, New York City, Ottawa, Montreal, Buenos Aires, Kinchasa (Congo), Jerusalem and Tel Aviv. The one fatality

* As shown by letters to *Time*, October 2, 1972. 'Once again, the legitimate interests of the Arab people have been betrayed—by Arabs.'
'If the Arabs have had an argument to which reasonable people would listen, it is now gone for ever.'

150

was the agricultural counsellor at Israel's London embassy. The letter bombs are sophisticated, difficult to detect and dangerous for even an expert to make. In some of those analysed the explosive was a powder, probably TNT; in others the charges were two thin strips of plastique about five inches long. Plastique is a mixture of Hexogen, TNT and rubber compound that can be moulded into any shape and is safe and stable until detonated. It can even be rolled sheet-thin to look like typewriter paper, written on, rolled or folded. If a letter bomb is torn open a tiny spring hits a detonator, little larger than an aspirin, which explodes the plastique. The whole thing can weigh less than an ounce and be scarcely an eighth of an inch thick. The lethal range is three feet. In other forms of letter bombs the act of opening the envelope or removing the 'letter' ignites a fuse or scratches a percussion cap that ignites the explosive. Others explode when the contents are exposed to air.

During 1972 the PFLP became as desperate—and as extreme—as Black September. The movement declared that pilgrims to the Holy Land of all ages and both sexes were legitimate targets and introduced a new tactic. On Tuesday May 30, 1972 a gang of three Japanese terrorists arriving at Lod Airport, Tel Aviv, by an Air France plane, fired submachine guns and lobbed hand-grenades into the crowded arrivals hall. They killed 24 people and wounded 57; 16 of the dead were Puerto Rican pilgrims. The Japanese suicide squad had been recruited by PFLP agents (though Black September fedayeen may also have been involved) earlier in the year and was trained in the mountains of southern Lebanon. They even visited Israel as tourists to study airport security arrangements before embarking on a plane at Rome.

Arab reaction to the massacre was joyful and King Hussein was the only leader to condemn it; he was also the only one to condemn the Munich massacre. Typical was the editorial of the Egyptian *Al-Akhbar* which exulted: '... Thus the myth that Israel is impregnable is shattered. Violence must breed violence....' In Lebanon, *Al-Yom* asked in a defensive tone: 'Why shouldn't the Arabs rejoice? We rejoice because Israel now realises that it is wide open to the will of the Arab international revolution....' *The Daily Star*, Beirut, explaining the psychology of the massacre: 'The Palestinians are drowning and will pull the whole world down with them.' *Al-Anwar* found satisfaction in Japanese involvement: 'The greatness of the Lod operation is reflected in the fact that the Palestinians were able to persuade the Japanese heroes to die for their cause. That was a shining proof that the cause of Palestine is alive in the hearts of free men in the world.'

The Japanese, members of an extremist Marxist or Maoist group in Japan, were denounced by their own country—which paid £1,500,000 voluntary compensation—and were said to be devotees of a suicide cult. That the PFLP has been forced to recruit Japanese fanatics to undertake suicide missions must reveal the difficulty it is having in persuading Palestinians to die for their own cause. Indeed, fewer and fewer students are prepared to join the movements; many of them rationalise their reluctance to join the ranks with: 'I'm too important to be endangered.'

Efforts to strike at Israel by infiltration and violence and by hijackings have assumed a symbolic character with the aim of preserving the spark of hope rather than doing actual damage. These activities do not mean that the conflict has entered a new, practical stage. Each act of terrorism arouses an Arab euphoria (the five fedayeen killed in Munich were hailed as martyrs) which quickly dissipates into disappointment at any lack of positive achievement. Despair, as a dialectical result, then strengthens tendencies to acquiesce to the situation. The Lod airport massacre is nothing more than an expression of despair within the PFLP itself.

The PFLP leaders implicitly conceded a degree of despair in a report as early as February 1969: 'The masses' evaluation of the enemy has been an emotional one. When partial successes are achieved the masses start to minimise the strength of the enemy and visualise the struggle as an easy and a quick one which will result in success in a short period. When the enemy directs heavy blows at the masses, they go to the other extreme and consider it a force which can never be defeated.'

There was despair in a statement by Abu Ayad in June that year: 'The Resistance movement now depends solely on itself ... the Arab mentality, education and experience are far from actually and effectively participating in solving the problems that they face.'* Despite such realisations, which have become stronger since 1969, the organisations cannot admit to themselves that each attack launched by their own or by hired assassins only further strengthens the Israelis. Also terrorism always reaches a point at which its excesses completely obscure the motive which inspired it. For this reason the Palestinians have fewer and fewer friends.

A leading Israeli general told me that if he were a Palestinian fedayeen leader fighting Israel he could make life intolerable for the Israelis. His statement was dispassionate and matter-of-fact and was intended to emphasise Arab inefficiency rather than his own, or Israeli, cleverness. What tactics he would use he did not specify; presumably he would apply the methods of the Jewish terrorists fighting the British. The Arabs are not capable of implementing such methods. Sir John Glubb has said, 'The guerrillas cannot, of course, drive out the Israeli army but they can make peace impossible.' This is tragically true, though if Egypt made peace there would be peace, regardless of the fedayeen. All the fedayeen can now do is to withhold peace from their own people who have so long craved it.

General Carl Van Horn, the Swede who commanded the UN peacekeeping force in the Middle East and who is no

* In an interview with Lutfi al-Khouli, editor-in-chief of the Egyptian monthly magazine, *Al-Tali'ah*, June 1969.

friend of the Israelis, describes fedayeen activities as 'political masturbation'. He would mean, in part, that the Palestinian organisations are poor substitutes for a real revolutionary force. To exist and operate they must make their peace with the Arab powers that be, in ways that a real revolutionary, such as Castro, would never do.

The observer is finally left with the conviction that the Palestinian fedayeen organisations—the force that never was—could more benefit their own people by going out of business altogether. But this will not happen. Resistance has become an industry, the fedayeen organisations have become entrenched bureaucracies in which the hierarchy are reluctant to eliminate their own authority.

In any case 'fedayeenism' is exportable and has become part of world violence. A Roman Catholic priest in Ulster denounced Vietnamese, Algerians and Palestinians working for the IRA who gave themselves a credibility cover by hanging crucifixes around their necks. Frustrated by failure in their natural theatre—the eastern Mediterranean area—the fedayeen will increasingly turn to targets in all continents.

By the end of 1972 rationality was no longer a factor in fedayeen thinking, except to the extent of reasoning that as nothing else worked in gaining their ends they would try havoc, and that any methods were justifiable. Fedayeenism is a way of life, a trade, and a state of mind, and in groups or as individuals fedayeen are likely to become more involved in the growth of urban guerrilla activity in other countries. Because of their experience, they are desirable collaborators and instructors.

Israel, and Israelis at home and abroad, will no doubt remain prime targets and inevitably more Israelis (among others of different nationalities) will be killed. But the real victims are, and must remain, the ordinary Palestinians.

Index

Abid, Ibrahim Al-, 100*n*, 124, 130
Abu Ayad, 2*n*, 5, 21, 31, 103, 130*n*, 147, 153
Abu Hassan, 148-9
Abu Sneima, deportation of terrorists' families to, 83
Aircraft, hijacking of, 45, 49, 52, 60-1, 78, 117, 147, 149-50; attacks on, 47-8, 72, 122; destruction of, 60
Al Ansar (Communist organisation), 78
Al-Ahram (Egyptian newspaper), 62-3, 99, 109
Algeria, supports fedayeen, 40-1, 67, 149; hijacking of plane to, 45; pacification policy of French in, 121; War of Independence, fedayeen war compared to, 92, 105-11
Al-Quds (Jerusalem Arab newspaper), 28, 113-14, 143
Alush, Naji, 106-7; *The March on Palestine of*, 10-11
Amman, fedayeen conflicts in, 44, 57-8, 60; recruitment in University of, 54; 'civil war' in, 61-3; base for Palestine liberation, 65; fedayeen leave, 67
Antonius, Soraya, 140
Arab: opposition to Fatah, 2, 11-13, 17-19; demand for 'liquidation' of Israel, 3, 8, 19, 88-9; violence against Jews, 5*n*; failure to write, 9-11; press and radio praise fedayeen activities, 14, 151-2; defeat in 1967, 23-4; self-esteem restored by Karamah, 31-2; Establishment PFLP's enemy, 37-8; doubts of fedayeen, 68, 133-5, 143; casualties in Gaza atrocities, 82-3; education in vengeance and brutality, 88-9, 95-8; financial support of fedayeen, 100; exaggeration of

fedayeen deeds, 102; condemnation of terrorist violence, 113-14; belief in Israeli technological wizardry, 130; lack of talent for guerrilla warfare, 131; exploitation of Palestinians, 138, 141
Arab Liberation Front, 29, 135
Arab Nationalists, 20, 42-3
Arab Women's Information Committee, 140
Arafat, Yasser, 5-7; Syria supports, 8, 15; and first Fatah venture, 12-14; meets Che Guevara, 16; Syria turns against, 18-19; and Six-Day War, 23; in Israeli-occupied territory, 24-7; Chairman of PLO, 34-5, 66; holds power in Jordan, 54, 58-9; his attitude to Palestinian State, 54, 144; Hussein makes terms with, 56, 62-3, 65-6; fails to get support against Hussein, 61; his analysis of conflict, 66; loses prestige, 70; makes pact with Lebanese Premier, 72-4; false claims of, 102-3; Israel's obsession with, 114; unnecessary publicity, 117; inconsistencies of, 118; Chinese arms for, 134; blamed for fedayeen failure, 143; mentioned, 10, 30, 45, 147
Armed Struggle Command (ASC), 35, 104, 141
'Arroyo' incident, 82-3
Ashbal, 'Lion Cubs', 96-8
Assad, Hafiz (Syrian Defence Minister), 19; President of Syria, 79, 134
Athens, PFLP terrorism in, 46, 48, 72
Auja, 'battle of', 104

Bakr, Ibrahim, 102

Fedayeen—(*Cont.*)
  Lebanese pressure on, 77-8; fight Arabs not Israelis in Gaza, 81-4; slogans of, 87, 91-4; accuse Israelis of 'torture of prisoners', 87, 123-5; lack realism, 93; casualties among, 94, 129; recruit by terror, 95; Junior, 96-8; lack knowledge of Israel, 98; finances and sponsors of, 99-100, 105; lose credibility, 101-12, 118; have no plans for a liberated Palestine, 110; fail to get secure bases, 110-11, 131; ignore what they do not want to know, 111-12; Western publicity for, 113-17; Israel bombs camps of, 116, 122-3; speak readily after capture, 123, 125; penalty in Israel for harbouring, 125-6; betrayed by own people, 126-7; Israel border defences against, 127-30; fundamental assumptions behind strategy of, 132; movement in decline, 132-42; attitude of Arab governments to, 134-6; despair among leaders of, 136, 140, 152-3; 'limited tasks' suitable for, 137; women, 138-41, 149; theories on cause of failure of, 143; desire among leaders of, for talks with Israel, 143-4; fall in numbers of, 146; desire revenge, 147; recruited in Europe, 149; Japanese terrorists recruited by, 152; organisations become bureaucracies and part of world violence, 154
Fifth of June Society, 140

Galilee, Israeli Arabs of, 95; defences near Sea of, 127-8
Gaza Strip, 80-6; refugees in, xiv, 80-1; fedayeen in, 5, 51, 80-5; Israeli occupation of, 5, 80; support for PLO in, 9; raids on Israel from, 16; UN Emergency Forces withdrawn from, 23; PFLP operations in, 49, 81-2; fedayeen terrorism in, 81-4, 139; included in bounds of Israel, 84; Israeli treatment of refugee camps in, 83, 85-6; Arab-occupied territory before 1967, 107
General Command of the Popular Front, 44
Germany, West, recruitment and training of Arab students in, 7, 15, 27; murder of Jordanians in, 70;

murder of Israeli athletes in, 77-8, 136, 150, 152; fedayeen cells in, 149
Ghadafi, Colonel, 135-6
Ghazawi, Said, 29
Golan Heights, 23-4, 128, 145
Guevara, Che, 16, 92, 111

Habash, George, 42-6, 66, 67; group of, 44, 46, 50, 52, 135; justifies PFLP tactics, 48-9; frustration of, 52; blackmail tactics of, 58; hijacks airliners, 60; reward for capture of, 63; false claims of, 102; blames failure on Arafat, 143; mentioned, 50, 59, 99, 117
Haddad, Wadi, 52, 60, 147
Halef, Salah (*see* Abu Ayad)
Harkabi, Dr. Yehoshafat, xiv, 24n, 92
Hashish smuggling, by Rasd, 149
Hawatmeh, Nayef, 44-5; accuses Habash and his group, 44; Group of, 44-5, 135; reward offered for capture of, 63; on cause of failures, 65, 143; mentioned, 46, 59, 117
Heikal, Mohammed, editor *Al-Ahram*, 109
Hermon, Mount, 71-2, 76, 145
Heroes of the Return, 20, 42-3
Hijacking operations, 45, 49, 52, 60-1, 78, 117, 147, 149-50
'Himmah' operations, 32
Hijazi, Mahmud Bakr, 16
'How an Armed Popular Revolution Breaks Out' (Fatah pamphlet), 16
Hussein, King of Jordan, opposes 'Palestinian entity', 8, 54; Syrian action against, 17; agrees to ceasefire with Israel, 24; opposes fedayeen, 53, 57, 59; deviation between words and actions of, 55-6, 59, 65-6; makes terms with Arafat, 56, 62-3, 65-6; humiliation of, 58; crushes and expels fedayeen, 61-7, 120, 134; justifies his action, 63-4; threat to, 147; condemns Lod massacre, 151

'Intellectuals of the Commandos', 55
IRA, fedayeenism in, 154
Iraq uses 'Palestinian entity' for own ends, 7-8; Fatah schools in, 40; and Jordan 'civil war', 62-3, 66; qualified support of, for fedayeen, 135; help from embassies of, 150